KEEP YOUR EYE ON THE BALL

The Science and Folklore of Baseball

KEEP YOUR EYE ON THE BALL

The Science and Folklore of Baseball

Robert G. Watts
A. Terry Bahill

W. H. FREEMAN AND COMPANY
NEW YORK

The cartoons on pages 25, 41, 57, 85, 135, 164, 180, and 195 are © 1990 by Sydney Harris.

Library of Congress Cataloging-in-Publication data

Watts, Robert G.
   Keep your eye on the ball : the science and folklore of baseball / by Robert G. Watts and A. Terry Bahill.
   p. cm.
   Includes bibliographical references (p.)
   ISBN 0-7167-2104-X ISBN 0-7167-2248 (pbk)
   1. Physics. 2. Baseball. 3. Force and energy. I. Bahill, A. Terry II. Title.
QC26.B38 1990
796.35701'53-dc20   89-49293
                                                                        CIP

To B, who hit us fly balls when he could; to Don, who caught them all gracefully and who hit me like a country cousin; and to Adam, who was developing a fair curve ball when he took up cycling instead.

RGW

To Alex and Zach, and all of our tolerant subjects.

ATB

CONTENTS

PREFACE

In 1982, one of us (Bob Watts) and two other scientists, Jim Walton of General Motors and Charlie Miller of MIT, had the privilege of photographing and analyzing a series of pitches thrown by Scott McGregor, a pitcher for the Baltimore Orioles, and Ray Miller, then the pitching coach for the Orioles. Miller, especially, was quite curious about what we were doing, and we had some lively, entertaining, and educational discussions. It has been our experience that baseball players, coaches, and fans alike are eager to discuss the science of baseball. They tend to be intelligent people who have some ideas of their own and are anxious to learn more about how science relates to their trade. These discussions spawned the writing of this book.

The book is written for the inquiring layperson or the fan who wonders if curve balls really curve (and, if they do, how and why), how knuckle balls and spitballs move, and how pitching a ball with backspin or overspin affects the batted ball.

Although there are self-styled pundits of the game who claim to know the answers to these questions, we take the approach that only by rigorously applying the laws of physics can these matters be resolved once and for all. Thus many controversial claims about the game are addressed and, we hope, resolved by this book.

The mere mention of the word *physics* may have a chilling effect on some readers. We have tried, therefore, to simplify the scientific discussions by using a minimal number of physical laws and equations. When we feel more scientific background might be helpful we provide boxes within the text so as not to interrupt the narrative of the discussion. We hope that, with a little concentration and adequate motivation, you will easily be able to understand the more technical aspects of analyzing the game of baseball.

Many people have given us advice and assistance while we were doing the research and writing this book. We would like to thank all of them, in particular Jerry Kindall and Jerry Stitt with the University of Arizona baseball team; Al Rosen, Cot Deal, Brett Butler, and Chris Speier of the San Francisco Giants; Branch Rickey, Brian Harper, Joe Orslak, and Nelson de la Rosa of the Pittsburgh Pirates Baseball Club; Mike

Candrea of the University of Arizona softball team; Steve Bahill of Tata's Machine Shop; Bill Karnavas, Udi Levine, and Yiannis Lauris of the University of Arizona; Pete Brancazio of Brooklyn College; Cliff Frohlich of the University of Texas; and, of course, our editor Jerry Lyons at W. H. Freeman and Company.

The Game of Baseball:

A Little History

*A*uthor Jacques Barzun is supposed to have said that anyone who wants to know the heart and mind of America had better know baseball. Why is baseball such a typically American game? Was it, as some folk history would have us believe, invented by the American Abner Doubleday on a field in Cooperstown, New York, in 1839? Or, rather, is it an outgrowth of an English game called *rounders*, whose rules were printed in *The Boy's and Girl's Book of Sports*, written by William Clarke[1] and originally published in London in 1829?

The claim that Abner Doubleday invented baseball began in 1889 at Delmonico's Restaurant in New York City. A group of several hundred people had gathered to honor a squad of professional baseball players who, under the leadership of Albert G. Spalding, president of the Chicago Baseball Club, had just returned from a world tour. At the time Spalding was spreading the gospel that baseball was America's national game. One speaker at the banquet, Abraham C. Mills, the fourth president of the National League, stated that he wanted it understood that patriotism and research had established that the game of baseball was American in origin.

Americans of the time would have found it difficult to admit that their favorite pastime was not American in origin. Many, however, including Henry Chadwick, one of the first great baseball sports writers, had claimed before the Delmonico's banquet — and still claimed after it — that American baseball had originated from the English game of rounders. Spalding, on the other hand, championed the American-origin theory. He finally met Chadwick's challenge by calling for a "blue ribbon commission" to be appointed, consisting of seven "men of high repute." The commission was a hand-picked crew made up of men who were at one time or another prominent in organized American baseball. One of these men was Abraham C. Mills. After three years of collecting testimony, Mills published a report in December, 1907, claiming that baseball had originated in the United States of America, and that the first method of playing it had been devised by General Abner Doubleday in Cooperstown, New York, in 1839. According to Mills, and to the testimony of Abner Graves, a childhood resident of Cooperstown, Doubleday had altered and thus improved a game similar to rounders called *town ball* by limiting the number of players and by requiring the game to be played by teams. Doubleday supposedly called his new game *baseball*. However, there is no indication in Doubleday's own writing that he had ever been interested in baseball, and in 1839 he was attending West Point, far from Cooperstown.

The Doubleday claim was given official confirmation in 1939, when the major leagues made elaborate preparations to commemorate the centennial of the game by establishing the Baseball Hall of Fame in Cooperstown. At that meeting a legislative committee of the state of New York put into evidence the proposition that Cooperstown, New York, was the birthplace of baseball. Furthermore, the Congress of the United States in the 1952 Celler report on baseball continued to maintain that baseball is a game of American origin, and to this day New York State officially claims Cooperstown as the place where Abner Doubleday created modern baseball. The Baseball Hall of Fame itself continues to make much of the so-called "Abner Doubleday baseball," an old ball supposedly found in a trunk by a descendent of Abner Graves, asserting that the ball once belonged to Graves and therefore must have been handled by Doubleday as well.

In spite of these claims — both official and unofficial — the term *baseball* had been known to both English and American boys long before Doubleday was born. In 1744 a book called *A Little Pretty Pocket Book*, published in London by John Newbery,[2] contained a rhyme describing the game of "Base-Ball" along with a picture illustrating the game. Newbery referred to cricket, town ball, and baseball as distinct games. This book was republished in several American cities in the late 1700's and was recently reprinted in 1967. Furthermore, according to Seymour,[3] there have been many references to ball games, including baseball, being played in America in the late eighteenth and early nineteenth century. George Ewing, a revolutionary war soldier, told in his journal of playing the game of "base" on April 7, 1778, at Valley Forge. Thurlow Weed, an upstate New York political boss, wrote in his autobiography that Rochester, New York, had a baseball club that played every afternoon during the ball season of 1825.

To be sure, these games of the eighteenth and early nineteenth century were different from the baseball played in the mid-1800's, just as the baseball played in the mid-1800's is different from modern baseball. Children of all ages, Americans and others, are ingenious devisers of sporting games. Many games similar to baseball have been played throughout the ages. Stickball, played in the streets of many of our cities, and the game of "red hot," played by boys and girls in country school yards, are games similar to baseball, but with the rules somewhat changed to accommodate the number of players, the size of the field, and the equipment available.

Rounders, town ball, and baseball appear to have been distinct games at least as early as 1744. The evolution of baseball as we know it probably occurred over many years and over a wide geographical area. Doubleday may or may not have been involved in the evolution, but he certainly did not *invent* either the game or the name.

◆ The Rules of the Game — Then ◆

Organized baseball as we now know it seems to have come out of men's clubs in the city of New York, specifically the Knickerbockers Baseball

KNICKERBOCKER NINE,
1864.

Club of New York, organized in about 1842 by a group of gentlemen.
The Knickerbockers was principally a social club with an exclusive
flavor similar to that of country clubs in the early 1900's. To the
Knickerbockers, a baseball game was simply a vehicle for amateur recre-
ation and polite social intercourse. The rules of the game emphasized
proper and polite conduct. The Knickerbockers apparently had the first
written rules of modern baseball. The ball was to weigh 6 to $6\frac{1}{4}$ ounces,
and to have a circumference of 10 to $10\frac{1}{4}$ inches (midway in size between
a modern baseball and a softball). It had an India-rubber center, and was
wound with yarn and covered with leather, much as is the ball of today.
A wooden bat of any length, but not over $2\frac{1}{2}$ inches in diameter at its
thickest part, was used. The players took their positions on a square
field with 90-foot baselines, three bases, and a home plate. The pitcher
stood 45 feet from the home base. For the first time, batters had to take
their turn in a regular rotation. Innings were over after three outs were
made, but games could last any number of innings. The first team to
score 21 runs was the winner. A batter was declared out if he swung at
and missed three pitches, provided the catcher caught the last one either
on the fly or on the first bounce. He was also out if a fair ball was caught
on the fly or a foul ball was caught on the fly or on the first bounce. An
important change was the elimination of the old practice of "soaking."
In the old games of rounders and town ball a batter was put out if he
was hit, or "soaked," by a ball thrown at him when he was off base. In
the Knickerbocker rules this was replaced with a new rule of putting out
the runner by touching him with the ball.

The pitching rules were closer to those of modern slow-pitch softball than to those of modern baseball. The pitcher had to toss the ball gently underhand as near to the plate as possible. The batter could ask for a high pitch or a low pitch, and decline to swing at as many as he wished. Integral were the post-game festivities, frequently including lavish dinner dances.

◆ *The All-American Sport* ◆

The early baseball clubs were restricted to high social classes. Baseball itself could hardly have remained so restricted, however, because the game was popular and inexpensive, and in the cities of the time there were many public parks and vacant lots. Part of baseball's present-day popularity lies, no doubt, in the timeliness of its origin. According to Betts,[4] the rise of the sport in America during the era of the Industrial Revolution is not coincidental. The most popular American sports of the early 1800's, horse racing, fishing, and fox hunting, were distinctly rural. By the middle of the century many of the white collar workers who lived in the rapidly expanding cities had become concerned about their sedentary lives. Hence, the emergence of baseball as an activity of the upper social classes. Easy access to inexpensive newspapers and the development of rail transportation led to rapidly increased interest in organized sports, both by participants and spectators. But why did baseball, as opposed to some other organized sport, emerge as America's national pastime? Horse racing was a popular spectator sport, but it did not allow mass participation. Basketball was not invented until 1892. Football has always been stigmatized by excessive brutality. As we have already said, baseball was inexpensive to play, and the availability of vacant lots and public parks made it easy for people to participate in the game. the rules were relatively easy to learn, and, in any case, most adults were familiar with them because they had played some version of the game in their childhood.

Above all, baseball is a sport where the fans can identify with the players, who appear to be men of average size and strength. To be sure, playing the game at its highest level requires tremendous skill, but in ways that can be emulated by most of us — at least in modest ways. Few have the hand–eye coordination of a Wade Boggs, but most of us can hit or catch a ball thrown or batted by one of our peers at the annual

Labor Day picnic. Football is dominated by men of extraordinary size and strength. Few can truly identify with the exploits of Lyle Alzedo or "Refrigerator" Perry. These are men who are fundamentally different from the rest of us. Similarly, basketball is dominated by exceptionally tall men. Larry Byrd displays considerable skill, but would this suffice if he were not nearly a foot taller than the average American male? In baseball no single person normally dominates. It is a true team sport. In basketball a Kareem Abdul Jabbar, while not by himself able to guarantee a championship, can make a tremendous difference to a team. In baseball each player must play his part, each must take his turn at hitting, and at fielding. Nobody participates in every play, except the pitcher and the catcher. Unless the batter strikes out, others must cooperate to get an out. Thus, cooperation and team play are of great importance. But most importantly, the game is played by men who at least appear to be physically normal.

Professional baseball players are not, of course, ordinary men. Consider, for example, the task that must be performed by a batter playing baseball in the major leagues. His task is to hit a 2.85-inch-diameter ball with a bat whose thicker end is 2.75 inches in diameter. The ball is thrown by a pitcher whose sole purpose is to prevent the batter from hitting the ball solidly. He throws the ball from a distance of 60 feet, 6 inches from the batter, and at speeds ranging from perhaps 70 to 100 miles per hour. More often than not, the ball is spinning at 2000 revolutions per minute and might be curving in one direction or another. The batter has perhaps half a second to decide to swing and to direct his bat to make a solid collision with the ball. Even if he hits it solidly, if the direction of the ball is such that an opposing player can either catch it before it reaches the ground or can relay the ball to first base before the batter runs there, the batter has failed in his task. If the batter succeeds just once in three tries, he is a star. Think of another sport in which that is true.

◆ *The Rules Change* ◆

Although the game the New York Knickerbockers played in the 1840's would be recognizable to today's baseball fan, both the rules of the game and the way it is played have undergone significant changes over the decades. In the early game, basemen actually played *on* the base, and the pitcher worked from a 6-foot-square box only 45 feet from home plate. The ball had to be thrown underhanded in such a manner that the hand always passed below the hip. The catcher stood some 20 feet behind the batsman without any of the protective devices used today. Indeed, no gloves or other protective devices were used by any of the players before about 1875. In that year the first glove, a skin-tight glove with the fingertips cut off, was reputedly worn by Charles C. Waitt, a first baseman for the St. Louis team. Catching was a tougher job then than it is today, especially after the catcher moved up closer to the batter to be in a better position to throw out runners trying to steal. In the 1870's the catcher's mask was introduced by Fred Thayer, the captain of the Harvard team. Before 1864, balls caught on the first bounce put the runner out. In that year the fly rule was introduced, requiring that for an out, batted balls must be caught on the fly. As the game became more than a polite exercise in sportsmanship, and winning became more important, players began to devise tricks to circumvent the rules. Dickie Pierce, a shortstop for the Atlantics, introduced bunting by gently tapping the ball in front of home plate and running to first base before the bewildered opponents could recover. For years this was considered unsportsmanlike, eliciting boos and catcalls from the fans. Fielders began dropping fly balls intentionally to convert an easy out into a double play. This necessitated the adoption of the infield fly rule. Basemen moved off their bases to better defensive positions. The art of backing up other fielders took hold. Sliding to avoid being tagged became common.

The rule-makers recognized early on, however, that the game was essentially a duel between the batter and the pitcher, and many of the rule changes reflected this. Pitchers began accumulating tricks to outwit the batters. Jim Creighton of the Brooklyn Stars and others began cheating on pitching style, which required the ball to be delivered with a stiff-armed, underhanded motion. Crieghton began speed pitching by adding an almost imperceptible wrist snap to his delivery. Creighton and Harry Wright initiated the change-up, a slow pitch thrown like a fastball. Then in the 1860's or 1870's the curve ball was introduced. The inventor of the curve will probably never be known for certain, although Arthur "Candy" Cummings may have been its originator. Cummings, who pitched for the Brooklyn Stars in the 1860's, is traditionally claimed to be the first pitcher to throw a curve ball, and a bust of him is in the Cooperstown hall of fame. However, Fred Goldsmith, an early pitcher, claimed that Charles Avery, a Yale player, invented the curve. Later, Goldsmith claimed he himself had invented the pitch. According to Robert Smith,[5] many pitchers in the 1860's were using the curve ball, but Cummings may have been the first to truly cultivate the pitch. Danzig and Reichler[6] state that Creighton was throwing the curve ball before 1862. Indeed, Henry Chadwick claimed that a Rochester pitcher, whose name he could not remember, was using the pitch as early as the 1850's. The curve ball may have had several independent inventors.

In the 1870's, as underhanded pitching improved, fans began to complain of dull, low-scoring games. Rule changes favoring the batter were instated to make the game more interesting to the fans. In 1879 the size of the pitcher's box was reduced to 6 by 4 feet, and the pitcher, as he started his motion, was required to face the batter. The number of balls required for a base on balls was reduced from 9 to 8. The batter would be called out on strikes if the catcher caught the third strike on the fly. This required the catcher to move closer to the plate. In 1881 the pitching distance was lengthened from 45 to 50 feet. In 1884 pitchers were allowed to throw with a shoulder-high motion, ushering in the era of overhand pitching. In 1885 the batters were aided when a rule was initiated allowing the use of a flat-sided bat. In 1886 the pitching box was enlarged to 7 by 4 feet. In 1887 batters were no longer given the privilege of requesting a high ball or a low ball. To compensate, four strikes were allowed if the third strike was a called strike, and a walk was counted as a hit. Batters hit by a pitched ball were given first base, and pitchers were forbidden to lift a foot until they actually delivered the ball. In 1893 the pitching distance was lengthened to the present distance of 60.5 feet. In 1893 the pitcher's rubber was introduced and the round bat was again required.

◆ A Tricky Pitch ◆

After these changes pitchers began to experiment with making the ball do tricks. According to Danzig and Reichler,[6] Billy Rhines of the Cincinnati Reds was the first to throw a rise ball, and Tom Ramsey was the originator of the sinker. Christy Matthewson later began to throw the screwball, a reverse curve that he called the fadeaway.

Elmer Stricklett in 1902 was the first to throw the spitball, a pitch he had apparently learned from George Hildebrand, an outfielder who was his teammate on the Sacramento Club. Stricklett himself later claimed that Frank Corridon of Providence began throwing it before he did.

Eddie Cicotte was the first pitcher to use the knuckle ball, according to Danzig and Reichler.[6] However, as with most other pitches, the real originator of the knuckle ball seems somewhat obscure. In *The Crooked Pitch*, Martin Quigley[7] says, " . . . pitchers tried their hand at the knuckle ball to replace the spitball that had been outlawed in 1919. But the origin of the knuckler goes way back. Ed Summers of the Detroit Tigers, who used it unsuccessfully in the games against the Cubs in the World Series of 1908, said he learned it from an old timer who threw it sidearm in the early '80's."

Possibly the earliest consistent practitioner of the knuckle ball in the major leagues was Ed Rommel of the Philadelphia Athletics. Rommel used the pitch to win 27 games for the seventh-place Athletics in 1922. Even after the spitball was outlawed in 1919, it continued to be used surreptitiously by major league pitchers. Quigley[7] provides a fine description of the spitball as well as of a host of other illegal pitches, including the mud ball, the shine ball, and the emery ball. He also provides a quote from Ray Miller, then the pitching coach of the Baltimore Orioles and one of the most colorful men in baseball. "Someday," said Ray, "I expect to see a pitcher walk out to the mound with a utility belt on—file, chisel, screwdriver, glue. . . . He'll throw the ball to the plate with bolts attached to it."

A favorite trick of the old-timers was to secretly use frozen baseballs when pitching to the opposing team. Stephen Hall[8] claims that "this is exactly what the good-pitch, no-hit Chicago White Sox used to do when hard-hitting teams came to town in the late 1950's." The coefficient of restitution, that is, the bounciness, of the India-rubber center of a baseball decreases rapidly as the temperature goes down. The frozen ball simply could not be hit as far.

◆ A Tricky Bat ◆

Hitters perform their mischief, too. The most common illegal act performed by the batter is the "doctoring" of the tool of his trade: the bat. A common trick is drilling a hole in the thicker end of the bat along its length and filling it with something light, typically cork. This makes the bat lighter and therefore easier to swing, producing faster bat speed and allowing better control. In Chapter 5 we discuss the effects of corking the bat. Former Yankee shortstop Tony Kubek claims that the players of his day used an ice pick to carve out the bat's dark grain which is the softer part of wood. They would then put pine tar in the grooves, let it harden, and resand it. This was supposed to give the bat a harder surface. There are also stories of players leaving the grooves in the bat after picking out the dark grain, thereby roughening the surface of the bat. The batter is less likely to foul the ball back or to hit a pop-up if the surface of the ball does not slip too much on the surface of the bat. Tampering with the bat in ways such as this is no longer officially allowed, but this does not mean that such things are no longer done.

Wet pine tar is a sticky substance that batters put on their bats to improve their grip. Placing pine tar beyond 18 inches from the small end of the bat is not allowed. In 1984 there was a controversy involving George Brett of Kansas City in a game against the New York Yankees. After Brett hit a home run, Yankee manager Billy Martin brought the bat to the umpire's attention, demonstrating that the pine tar had gone beyond the 18-inch legal limit. The homer was nullified. American League president Lee McPhail later reinstated the homer, saying the rule was intended simply to keep the ball clean. George Brett probably knew better.

◆ Baseball and Science ◆

Baseball players are constant practitioners of applied physics. Each time a pitcher throws a ball or a batter alters the surface of his bat, he is putting the laws of physics to work for his benefit. Once you have read the remainder of this book, you will have a better understanding of how this is done.

Notes

1. William Clarke, *The Boy's and Girl's Book of Sports*, J. S. Hammond, Providence, 1841. An early book about sporting games for children.
2. J. Newbery, *A Little Pretty Pocket Book*, Harcourt, Brace, and World, New York, 1967. A book of sports games first published in the eighteenth century.

3. H. Seymour, *Baseball*, Oxford University Press, 1960.

4. J. R. Betts, *America's Sporting Heritage*, Addison-Wesley, Reading, Mass., 1974. A scholarly book on the history of sports in the United States.

5. R. Smith, *Baseball*, Simon and Schuster, New York, 1947.

6. A. Danzig and J. Reichler, *The History of Baseball*, Prentice-Hall, Englewood Cliffs, N. J., 1959. This book contains interesting historical notes, good photographs, and anecdotal stories about great teams and individual players.

7. M. Quigley, *The Crooked Pitch: An Account of the Curve Ball in American Baseball*, Algonquin Books, Chapel Hill, N.C., 1984.

8. Steven S. Hall, "Baseball's Dirty Tricks," *Science 83*, vol. 4, no 8, August 1983, pp. 92–93. How players get around the rules.

Also of interest:
P. Dickenson, *The Dickenson Baseball Dictionary*, Facts on File, New York, 1989.

The Flight of the Ball:

Do Curve Balls Curve?

"*A* curve ball," says Baltimore Orioles pinch-hitter Terry Crowley, "comes straight in, then about four or five feet from home plate, it breaks straight down." "It doesn't look like the ball starts breaking until about ten feet away," agrees Oriole catcher Joe Nolan. According to W. F. Allman,[1] Rich Dauer of the Orioles doesn't believe it: "A curve is a big swoop. It's like you have a rock on a string and you swing it. It goes out, and it curves in. Like you drew it with a compass. It's always the same rainbow."

Sandy Koufax's curve ball has been described as looking like it rolled off a table. Legend has it that Walter Johnson could make his fastball rise, appearing to defy the law of gravity. The flights of curve balls and "rising" fastballs, as well as many other pitches — legal and illegal — are the subjects of much baseball folklore. Does a baseball curve? If so, does it fly in the "rainbow" arc described by Dauer, or does it "break," as many hitters believe? Is a "rising" fastball possible, even when the man throwing it is the great Walter Johnson?

It may be especially surprising to those of you who have hit (or swung at) a well-thrown curve ball that there has not always been universal agreement on whether a ball curves at all, let alone whether it "breaks" or curves in a rainbow arc. According to Allman,[1] "In an 1870 demonstration Fred Goldsmith reportedly threw a sidearm curve at three upright poles arranged in a straight line. The ball traveled to the right of the first, to the left of the second, and to the right of the third," thus proving that a curve ball curves. Will White of the old Cincinnati Red Stockings, "one of the league's best righthanders," reportedly accomplished this same feat in 1877, as Einstein[2] tells it. Still doubts persisted. A Professor Stoddard, of Worcester University, in Massachusetts, wrote in the *Cincinnati Inquirer* shortly after White's demonstration, that "it is not only theoretically but practically impossible for any such impetus to be conveyed to a moving body as would be required . . . to control the movement of what is termed a curve ball."

In 1941 the controversy began anew, when an old baseball scout claimed that there was no such thing as a curve ball, and that everyone in baseball knew it (see Einstein[2]). This story was contained in a letter to *The New Yorker* magazine from R. W. Madden,[3] in which he recounted a conversation with an elderly gentleman who claimed to be a major-league scout, and who asked not to be named because "the guys in baseball have an interest in keeping the secret. It makes the game exciting to have curves . . .." and "In the second place, some guys might be willing to say they doubted if there was such a thing as curves, only what would happen to 'em? I'll tell you. They'd be laughed out of town." The response from readers lasted for several months. Noel Houston[4] wrote that he recalled that Dick Rover, a fictional character in the famous Rover Boys books, had "proved" to an elderly professor that curve balls do curve by throwing a curve ball through a series of wooden frames covered with dampened tissue paper. When the frames were later laid on top of one another, they showed clearly that the ball had traveled in a straight line until it neared home plate, after which the sudden veering of the positions of the holes traced the break of the ball. Lucy Stanton[5] wrote that her father had seen a demonstration by Tommy Bond, a pitcher with the Boston Baseball Club. Bond threw a curve ball that weaved between three stakes just as Fred Goldsmith and

Will White were supposed to have done; this demonstration was also reported by Smith.[6] However, Ray Lillibridge[7] disputed all these experiments, reporting that one man, after attending such a demonstration, suggested that "we were hypnotized . . . [because] the human eye could not detect which side of a stake an object the size of a baseball traveling at that speed had passed."

◆ A Picture's Worth A Thousand Words ◆

In the same year (1941) that Lillibridge disputed the feasibility of detecting curve balls, *Life* magazine[8] picked up the gauntlet. The magazine's high-speed photographer, Gjon Mili, using high-speed stroboscopic lighting at night, positioned three cameras to photograph balls thrown by two pitchers: Cy Blanton of the Philadelphia Phillies and Carl Hubbell of the New York Giants. The conclusions drawn from the resulting photographs were that Blanton's "best curve is really a straight ball with a decided drop," and that "Hub threw everything in his pitching book" and "wound up with . . . two straight lines." Although the publishers failed at the time to recognize the fact, the pictures published in *Life* magazine are the first hard proof of the existence of the curve ball. The pictures taken by Mili are shown in Figure 1. Once we have set the stage with a little background science, we will return our attention to these pictures and discover why they prove the existence of the curve ball.

◆ The Laws of Motion ◆

Before we begin our analysis of the curve ball, let's first look at a simpler situation. Our everyday experience tells us that objects such as the ball in Figure 2 will not move unless pushed or pulled, that is, unless acted on by a *force*. We call this tendency of objects at rest to remain at rest *inertia*. One measure of inertia is *mass*. The greater the mass of a body, the greater will be its tendency to remain at rest.

Now let's analyze what happens to the ball when it is moving at a constant speed toward the other end of the table. If we neglect for the moment the effects of friction between the ball and the table, the ball

FIGURE 1. *The first attempt to use photography to prove that a curve ball really curves was done by* Life *magazine in 1941. The balls shown here were photographed at night using stroboscopic lighting, giving a series of stop-action photos of the baseball. At the left is a pitch considered a curve ball and at the right a pitch considered a screwball, both thrown by Carl Hubbell of the New York Giants. The editors of* Life *concluded that neither ball curved, since both trajectories appear to lie in a plane. (Photographs, Gjon Mili* Life *Magazine © 1941 Time Inc.)*

FIGURE 2. *A ball with a smooth surface sitting on a level table will not move unless acted on by a force.*

FIGURE 3. *The ball rolling across the table will maintain its uniform motion.*

will maintain its *uniform motion* as it rolls across the table. As the length of the arrows in Figure 3 indicate, it will tend to maintain the same speed at which it started its journey.

These observations can be summarized as follows.

> Unless pushed or pulled, an object or body in a state of rest will tend to remain at rest. Likewise, a body in motion at a particular speed and in particular direction will tend to maintain the same speed and travel in the same direction.

Now let's see what happens when we push the moving ball from another direction. As Figure 4 shows, both its speed and direction of motion will change. With this observation, our previous statement can be qualified:

> A body at rest or in a state of uniform motion in a straight line will remain at rest or maintain its speed and direction of motion unless acted on by a force.

Although our observations of the ball's motion may not seem to be very important, they constitute one of the most fundamental laws in physics. In fact, it is called the first law of motion. It was first formulated by the seventeenth-century physicist Isaac Newton, who was the first to recognize its fundamental applicability to almost every aspect of the physical universe. To honor this scientific genius, it is also called *Newton's first law of motion.*

FIGURE 4. *When the rolling ball is pushed from another direction, both its speed and direction of motion are changed.*

We have been talking about the speed and direction of a moving body. In physics, however, the quantity *velocity* is used to describe these two aspects of motion. Thus we speak of a velocity of 80 miles per hour *due east*. One way to graphically show the velocity of a moving object is to use a *vector*. (See boxes, pages 19 and 20.) In Figure 5, the arrows are vectors representing the velocity of the ball at points A and B. The lengths of the arrows indicate the magnitudes of the velocities, that is, the speed of the ball at points A and B, while the directions in which the arrows point indicate the directions of motion of the ball at each point.

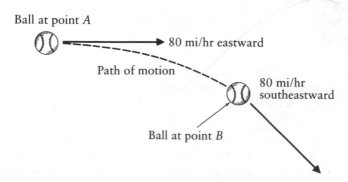

FIGURE 5. *Although the ball is moving at the same* speed *at points* A *and* B, *its velocity has changed because velocity is a* vector. *A vector has both magnitude and direction, and the direction of the velocity vector changed as the ball traveled from point* A *to point* B.

Vectors

A quantity that can be specified by a magnitude only is called a *scalar*. If a particle undergoes a change in its position, its new position and old position are related by two quantities, the distance between the two quantities, and the direction of the second position relative to the first. The change in position is called *displacement*. It has both magnitude and direction. It can be represented by drawing an arrow from the first position (position A, below) to the second position (position B). The length of the arrow represents the distance or the *magnitude*, of the displacement.

If the particle subsequently moves to another position (position C in the figure below), the displacement from B to C can be constructed by drawing an arrow from B to C. Furthermore, the total displacement from A to C can be represented by an arrow drawn from A to C. The sum of the first two arrows is represented by the third arrow. Quantities that behave like this are called *vectors*.

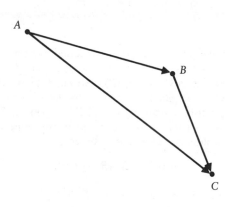

✕ Adding and Subtracting Vectors ✕

Let us see how the displacement vector between points B and C can be added to give the displacement vector between points A and C. First we name the displacement from A and B $\mathbf{D}(AB)$ and the displacement from B and C $\mathbf{D}(BC)$. We use boldface type to represent the vectors $\mathbf{D}(AB)$ and $\mathbf{D}(BC)$. The directions of the two vectors are specified by the two angles $\theta(AB)$ and $\theta(BC)$ in the

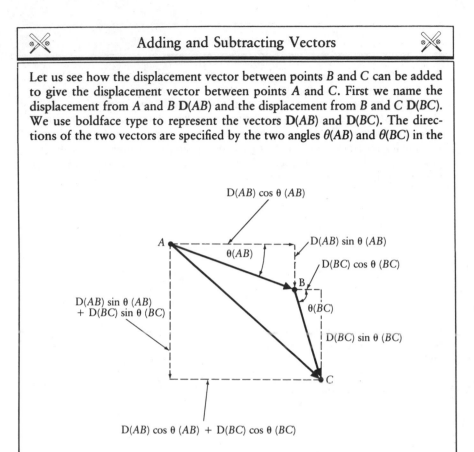

figure above. Because of the way vectors are added, we can represent $\mathbf{D}(AB)$ by the sum of the two vectors with magnitudes $\mathbf{D}(AB) \cos \theta(AB)$ pointing in the horizontal direction and $\mathbf{D}(AB) \sin \theta(AB)$ pointing downward. These are called components of the vector. Similarly, the vector $\mathbf{D}(BC)$ can be represented by $\mathbf{D}(BC) \cos \theta(BC)$ pointing to the right and $\mathbf{D}(BC) \sin \theta(BC)$ pointing downward. Now colinear vectors (vectors pointed in the same or opposite directions) can be added directly. Therefore, the vector

$$\mathbf{D}(AC) = \mathbf{D}(AB) + \mathbf{D}(BC)$$

has a horizontal component $\mathbf{D}(AB) \cos \theta(AB) + \mathbf{D}(BC) \cos \theta(BC)$ and a vertically downward component of magnitude $\mathbf{D}(AB) \sin \theta(AB) + \mathbf{D}(BC) \sin \theta(BC)$.

Another important vector quantity is acceleration. As we know only too well from our personal experiences on public transportation or on the highway, acceleration is a rate of change in the velocity of a moving body. Thus, if a train traveling south at 40 miles per hour changes its speed to 60 miles an hour in 2 seconds, it experiences an average *acceleration* of 20 miles per hour per 2 seconds, or 10 mi/h/s in the direction of south. The acceleration is the rate at which the velocity changes with time. Thus, the average acceleration experienced by the ball in Figure 5 is the change in the velocity vector divided by the time required to go from point A to point B. (See box, page 22.)

Keep in mind that a change in acceleration does not always require a change in the speed of an object. For example, although the speed of the ball at points A and B in Figure 6 is the same, the direction in which the ball is traveling is different at each point. Thus the velocity of the ball has changed in going from point A to point B—that is, the ball has accelerated.

FIGURE 6. *Although the speed of the ball is the same at points A and B, the directions of motion and thus the velocities are different.*

⚔ Acceleration ⚔

Let's examine the method of calculating the acceleration experienced by the ball in Figure 5. The ball is initially moving at 80 mph to the east and at a later time is moving at 80 mph to the southeast, that is, at an angle 45° below a horizontal line in the figure. We will assume that a period of time of 10 seconds has elapsed while the ball moved from position A to position B. The velocity at **B** is the vector **V**(B) and the velocity at A is the vector **V**(A). Since the average acceleration is the velocity difference divided by the time elapsed,

$$\mathbf{a} = \frac{\mathbf{V}(B) - \mathbf{V}(A)}{t(B) - t(A)}$$

The figure below shows that the velocity difference is a vector with components 80(1 − cos 45°) = 23.4 mph to the left and 80 sin 45° = 56.6 mph downward. The magnitude of this acceleration can be determined by the use of the Pythagorean theorem, which states that the magnitude of the hypotenuse of a right triangle is equal to the square root of the sum of the squares of the sides, or $\sqrt{(23.4)^2 + (56.6)^2}$ = 61.2 mph. The direction is specified by the angle θ shown in the figure. It is the angle whose tangent is 23.4/56.6 = 0.429, or θ = 23.2°. The acceleration is therefore 61.2 mph/10s, or 6.12 mi/hr/s in the direction 90° − 23.2°, or 66.8° south of due west.

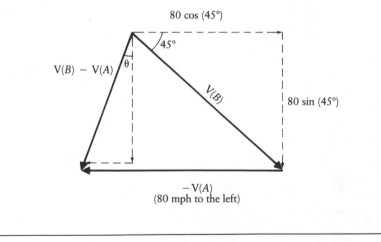

Finally, one more important vector quantity is force. When we want to specify the force experienced by an object, we must use a vector to indicate not only the size of the force but also the direction in which it acts. Since weight is a force experienced by all material bodies on Earth, it must be graphically represented by a vector, a vector pointing toward Earth. Now that we are armed with this background, let's return to the ball rolling on the table.

FIGURE 7. *The two forces acting on the rolling ball.*

As Figure 7 shows, there are two forces acting on the rolling ball. One is the force of gravity. This force pulls the ball downward toward the ground. We call this the *weight* of the ball, and give it the symbol w. Since the ball does not move toward the ground, there must also be a force equal in strength pushing up on the ball. This force is exerted by the table surface on the ball. As the figure shows, these two forces are equal in strength but opposite in direction and thus cancel one another. That is, there is no *net* force on the ball. According to Newton's first law, therefore, it will continue to roll at the same speed and in the same direction.

Suppose the ball rolls off the surface. The upward force exerted by the surface on the ball will not be present, and our experience tells us that the ball will be accelerated downward, or fall, because it experiences an *unbalanced* force, the weight of the ball. To understand the resulting motion, we again turn to Newton for another law of motion:

> The acceleration of a body that is acted on by a net force is inversely proportional to its mass and directly proportional to the net force acting on it.

This is called the *second law of motion* or *Newton's second law*. (See box, page 24.)

Now, when the ball falls off the table, the only force acting on it is its weight w (neglecting, for now, the resistance of the air as it rushes past the ball). In accordance with the second law, the downward speed of the ball begins to increase; that is, the ball experiences an acceleration.

Newton's Second Law

A mathematical description of Newton's second law of motion is

$$\mathbf{F} = m\mathbf{a}$$

The force $\mathbf{F}$ (a vector) is equal to the mass m of an object (a scalar) multiplied by its acceleration $\mathbf{a}$ (a vector). Since $m\mathbf{a}$ and $\mathbf{F}$ are both vectors and are equal, they must have both the same magnitude and the same direction. The force on the ball referred to in Box 3 must have been directed 66.8° south of due west. Its magnitude could be calculated simply by multiplying the mass of the ball by the magnitude of the acceleration.

What is the amount of this acceleration? To find out, we turn to the sixteenth-century astronomer and experimental philosopher, Galileo Galilei. Galileo discovered, long before Newton's time, that the acceleration experienced by a body dropped from above the Earth is constant. (Actually, this value changes depending on the elevation of the body above the surface of the Earth, but for our purposes the variation is small.) This constant acceleration is given the special symbol, g and is equal to 32 feet per second for each second the ball falls. For example, after 1 second the ball will be traveling at a downward speed of 32 feet per second. After another second the ball's downward speed will have gained another 32 feet per second, so that its speed will be 64 feet per second. And so on.

Eventually, of course, the drag of the air rushing past the ball will produce a force equal and opposite to the weight of the ball and, again in accordance with the first law, the ball will cease accelerating and fall at a constant velocity. This is, for example, the principle of a parachute. The greatly exposed area of the parachute's fabric serves to increase the drag force to a value high enough that a human can fall from great height and reach a "free fall" velocity small enough to prevent injury on landing. The free-fall velocity of a baseball in air is about 150 feet per second. As we shall see later, this aerodynamic drag force on a baseball is by no means unimportant, at least for long fly balls. For our present "thought experiments," however, let us agree to neglect it. We will add it to our analysis later, after our understanding of the basic laws of motion is more nearly complete.

Having analyzed the concepts of force (a push or a pull) and acceleration (the rate at which velocity increases), we can now set about understanding mass. As we have said, the downward force on a falling ball is its weight w. Falling under the influence of gravity, the ball will accelerate at a rate given by g. Newton's second law tells us that the weight of the ball is equal to the mass of the ball multiplied by the acceleration due to gravity g:

$$w = mg$$

Far from the Earth or from any other body, the force of gravity becomes zero and an object becomes weightless. Since there are no forces on the object, its acceleration is also zero. Its mass, however, remains the same wherever the body is. If an object is placed on the surface of the Moon, it weighs about one sixth as much as it does on the surface of the Earth, because the acceleration of gravity on the Moon is one sixth that at the surface of the Earth. The *mass* is the same whether the object is on the Earth or the Moon or in outer space. It is equal to the weight of the object wherever it is, divided by the gravitational acceleration at that location;

$$m = \frac{w}{g}$$

According to Newton's second law of motion, an object under the influence of a constant force undergoes a constant acceleration that is directly proportional to the size of the force and inversely proportional to the mass of the object. Galileo guessed, and then verified experimentally, that the resulting motion of the object would be such that the distance traveled by the object would be proportional to the square of the time t. This result was later shown to be a direct result of Newton's laws of motion. The mathematical statement is

Distance travelled $= 1/2$ (acceleration)(time)(time)

or

$$d = 1/2\ at^2$$

Let us now return to our thought experiment about the ball rolling off the top of a table. Once the ball leaves the surface it is influenced by a vertical force, the force of gravity, or the weight of the ball. There is no horizontal force on the ball. There is a corollary to Newton's laws that tells us that as long as the horizontal and vertical forces on the ball are not dependent on one another, we can treat their effects separately. The total effect on the ball will be the combined effects of the vertical and horizontal forces. Suppose the ball rolls off the table at 50 feet per second without a horizontal force on the ball (remember: we are neglecting drag by the air). It will continue at a horizontal speed of 50 feet per second and, after 1 second, will be 50 feet from the edge of the surface. Its vertical (downward) displacement increases according to the preceding equation, where a is the acceleration due to gravity, 32 ft/s^2. After 1 second it will have fallen a distance $d = 1/2\ (32)(1)^2 =$

16 feet. After 2 seconds, it will have traveled $2 \times 50 = 100$ feet horizontally and $1/2 \, (32)(2)^2 = 64$ feet downward; after 3 seconds, $50 \times 3 = 150$ feet horizontally and $1/2 \, (32)(3)^2 = 144$ feet downward, and so on.

Figure 8 illustrates what we have described. The first picture shows the horizontal motion alone, the middle picture shows the vertical motion alone, and the last picture shows the actual motion of the ball, a combination of the horizontal and vertical motions. Using vector arithmetic (see box, page 30), we find that the speed of the ball 1 second $(t = 1)$ after falling from the table is $\sqrt{(50)^2 + (16)^2}$, or about 52 feet per second in the direction shown.

We are now equipped to analyze the motion of a pitched or batted ball. Suppose that instead of rolling off a flat surface, the ball is thrown with a vertical velocity of 50 feet per second and also a horizontal velocity of 50 feet per second. If we were somehow able to turn off the force of gravity (or do our experiment on a space platform where there is no gravity), there would be no force on the ball and it would travel along the straight dashed line shown in Figure 9. The speed of the ball would be $\sqrt{(50)^2 + (50)^2}$, or about 71 feet per second, at an angle of 45 degrees from the horizontal. When gravity is present, the ball will fall *below this line* by the distances indicated in the figure and calculated from the equation $d = 1/2 \, at^2$ for $t = 1, 2, 3, 4$, and 5. After 1 second, it will be 16 feet below the dashed line. After 2 seconds it will be 64 feet below the dashed line. Eventually, of course, the ball will hit the ground.

The curve described by the path of the ball shown in Figure 9 is called a *parabola* or *parabolic arc*. There is a simple mathematical expression for this arc. Let us agree to call the vertical distance from where the ball is thrown z, the horizontal distance x, the initial vertical velocity v_{z0}, and the initial horizontal velocity v_{x0}. The vertical distance, or height of the ball, at time t is just the difference between where it would be if gravity were absent, $z_1 = v_{z0} \, t$, and the distance through which it has fallen due to its weight when gravity is present, $z_2 = 1/2 \, gt^2$:

$$z = v_{z0} \, t - 1/2 \, gt^2$$

The horizontal distance traveled by the ball at time t is

$$x = v_{x0} \, t$$

By solving the second equation above for t and substituting this into the first equation we can find the relation between z and x, from which

FIGURE 8. *(Top) The motion of a moving ball if there were no gravitational force. (Middle) If the ball had no initial horizontal or vertical velocity, it would* accelerate *downward under the force of gravity (the weight of the ball) and in the last position shown have a velocity* v_z. *(Bottom) If the ball rolls off the table with some initial horizontal speed* v_x *the two effects described above act together.*

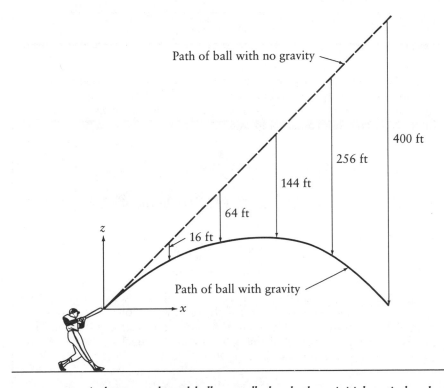

Path of ball with no gravity

400 ft

256 ft

144 ft

64 ft

16 ft

Path of ball with gravity

FIGURE 9. *A thrown or batted ball normally has both an initial vertical and an initial horizontal speed as it leaves the player's hand or bat. If there were no gravitational force and no air resistance, the ball would continue to move in its initial direction with the same speed (dashed lines). Under the force of gravity (but neglecting air resistance), the ball falls below this straight line at an accelerating rate (solid line). The actual path of the ball is a parabola lying in a vertical plane.*

we can derive an equation giving us the range R of the ball—that is, the horizontal distance the ball travels before returning to the height from which it was thrown. (See box, page 30.)

We now consider one last thought experiment with our fictitious ball. Until now we have studied the motion of a ball that had an initial velocity and subsequently was subjected to a single force, the weight of the ball. The resulting motion of the ball could be visualized in a single plane, the x-z plane (see Figure 9). This motion is called *planar* or *two-dimensional* motion. We now imagine the motion of a ball when there is another force on the ball, in a direction mutually perpendicular to the x and z directions. We name this the y direction, and the motion

---

⚔   Equation for Range   ⚔

When the drag on a moving object due to the presence of air is negligibly small, its horizontal velocity remains constant. The last equation on page 27 tells us that the time required to move horizontally a distance x is the distance divided by the (constant) horizontal speed v_{x0}:

$$t = \frac{x}{v_{xo}}$$

This expression of time can be substituted for t in the equation $z = v_{z0}t - \frac{1}{2}gt^2$, with the result

$$z = v_{z0}\left(\frac{x}{v_{xo}}\right) - \frac{1}{2}g\left(\frac{x}{v_{xo}}\right)^2$$

Notice that when $x = 0$ in this equation, $z = 0$. This simply states that the ball was at the horizontal position $x = 0$ and the vertical position $z = 0$ at the same time. This was at time $t = 0$, of course. At some time later $z = 0$ again. This occurs when the two terms on the right side of the equal sign in the above equation are equal to one another, or when

$$v_{zo}\left(\frac{x}{v_{xo}}\right) = \frac{1}{2}g\left(\frac{x}{y_{xo}}\right)^2$$

and this occurs when

$$x = \frac{2v_{xo}v_{zo}}{g}$$

This value of x is called the range of the ball—the horizontal distance it will travel from the time it leaves the ground until it reaches the ground again.

---

is what we call *three-dimensional motion*. Imagine now a ball leaving the origin of the coordinates (the place where the three coordinate lines come together, that is, where x, y, and z are all 0). The ball has an initial velocity v_{z0} in the vertical (z) direction, an initial velocity v_{x0} in one horizontal (x) direction, and no initial velocity in the other horizontal (y) direction. There is a vertical force, the weight of the ball, pulling downward, in the z direction. As before, we can treat the three effects separately. The distances the ball travels in the z and x directions are unchanged from our previous thought experiment. However, the ball is now subjected to a force in the y direction, which we denote as F_y. Hence, according to Newton's second law, it will have an acceleration in the y direction of

$$a_y = \frac{F_y}{m}$$

and, since $m = w/g$, this acceleration can be expressed as

$$a_y = \frac{F_y}{w} g$$

According to the equation $d = \frac{1}{2} at^2$, it will move in the y direction as

$$y = \frac{1}{2} \left[\frac{F_y g}{w} \right] t^2$$

Equation $x = v_{x0}t$ can be solved for t and the equation above can be solved for t^2 and the results substituted into the equation so that $z = v_{z0}t - \frac{1}{2} gt^2$,

$$z = \left[\frac{v_{z0}}{v_{x0}} \right] x - \left[\frac{w}{F_y} \right] y$$

This is an important result. It is the equation of a plane. This plane is shown in Figure 10.

◆ *The Equation of a Plane* ◆
and the Curve Ball's Path

What does this equation have to do with the existence of a curve ball? We first analyzed the trajectory of a ball that was subjected only to one force after it was thrown: a vertical (downward) force equal to the weight of the ball. The ball moved in a parabolic arc in a plane, the x-z plane. We have now shown that if the ball additionally experiences a horizontal force perpendicular to the x-z plane (that is, in the y direction in Figure 10), the ball still travels in a parabolic arc in a plane, but the plane, instead of being vertical, slopes in the y direction. *This can happen only if there is a horizontal force in the y direction.*

We have just described the path of a curve ball, of course. Figure 10 shows how a curve ball loops in the parabolic arc due to the force of gravity, but also moves in the y direction. Compare it with the pictures from *Life* magazine in Figure 1. The balls thrown by Carl Hubbel and shown in the figure are not moving in vertical planes, but in planes sloping to one side or the other. Clearly, there are horizontal forces on

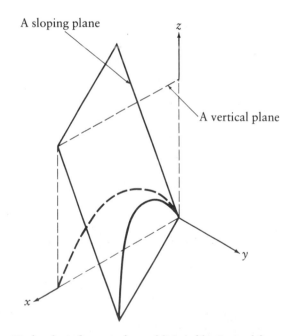

FIGURE 10. *Under the influence of an additional horizontal force perpendicular to the initial direction of travel, the ball will accelerate in this horizontal direction (the Y direction in this figure). The ball moves in a parabolic arc, but not in a vertical plane. Instead, it moves in a plane sloping downward and in the direction of the extra force. Comparison of this drawing with the* Life *magazine photograph (Figure 1) of Carl Hubbell's curve ball shows how that photograph proves Hubbell's pitch did indeed curve.*

these pitches. These photographs were indeed the first concrete proof of the existence of the curve ball!

◆ *The Laws of Motion and Pitched Baseballs* ◆

Let us now investigate some quantitative aspects of pitched baseballs and get accustomed to using the equations we have just derived. There are many interesting questions that can be answered before proceeding any further with theory.

Consider Dwight Gooden's fastball. Let's suppose it is thrown horizontally at 100 miles per hour and has no forces on it other than the downward pull of gravity. We will assume for simplicity that the ball travels 60 feet between the time it is thrown and the time it reaches home plate. (The distance to home plate from the pitcher's rubber is 60 feet 6 inches, but the ball only travels about 55 feet in the air because of the pitcher's arm and stride. We will use 60 feet throughout this book for consistency and simplicity.) We can compute how long the ball is in the air by using equation $x = v_{x0}t$. The ball travels a horizontal distance x at a horizontal speed v_{x0} in an amount of time

$$t = \frac{x}{v_{x0}}$$

We first express the speed in feet per second. Since there are 5,280 feet in a mile and 3,600 seconds in an hour, 100 miles per hour equals $(100)(5200)/(3600) = 147$ feet per second. The time required to reach the strike zone is therefore

$$t = \frac{60 \text{ ft}}{147 \text{ ft/s}} = 0.41 \text{ s}$$

The batter has only about four-tenths of a second to decide whether the pitch will be in the strike zone and to swing his bat in such a way as to make an effective collision with the ball. Not many people can throw a baseball as fast as Dwight Gooden. An 85-mile-per-hour fastball has helped many a major league pitcher earn a good living. Such a pitch takes $(0.41)(100/85) = 0.48$ seconds to reach the strike zone. A 70-mile-an-hour fastball will be hammered out of the park by many high school players. Yet it reaches the strike zone in 0.58 seconds, only about one tenth of a second slower than a major league fastball. Ten to fifteen hundredths of a second is all that separates you and me from multimillion dollar careers in major league baseball!

If a ball is thrown horizontally at 100 miles per hour (147 feet per second), how far will it fall vertically before crossing home plate? To do this computation, we can use equation $z = v_{z0}t - \frac{1}{2}gt^2$. Since the ball is thrown horizontally, $v_{z0} = 0$. The time required for the flight of the ball is 0.41 second, and the acceleration of gravity g is 32 feet per second per second. The vertical displacement is therefore

$$z = -\tfrac{1}{2}(32)(0.41)^2 = -2.69 \text{ ft}$$

or 2.69 feet downward. Even a ball thrown at the tremendous speed of a Dwight Gooden (or a Walter Johnson or a Bob Feller . . .) fastball drops by over $2\frac{1}{2}$ feet during its flight to home plate. In order to make a pitch rise, of course, some external upward force must operate on the ball. The magnitude of this force must be larger than the weight of the ball. *Any* upward force, however, would cause the ball to *rise above the parabolic arc* depicted in Figure 10. Since we are accustomed to seeing things move in these parabolic arcs, it seems entirely possible that departures from these arcs would be "seen" by a batter as a rise in the path of the ball. Or, maybe they do rise. Let's not decide this until we've had a chance to investigate the origins and magnitudes of forces that can be imposed on the ball by skillful pitchers.

For now, suppose a sideward force *can* somehow be put on the ball. How far will the ball curve on the way to home plate? First of all, to see what we mean by "how far," refer to Figure 11. This drawing is similar to that in Figure 10, except that a little more detail has been added. If we looked down from directly above the pitcher, and without depth perception, we would see the projection of the path of the ball in the *x-y* plane. By drawing vertical lines from the positions of the ball at several values of time, and marking where these lines cross the *x-y* plane, we can get an idea of the path we would see from our position above the pitcher. The ball is curving, or moving in the *y* direction, because there is a force in that direction. Its acceleration in the *y* direction is given by the first two equations on page 31. The distance the ball moves away from the *x*-axis (the direction in which it was thrown) is given by the third equation. When we speak of how far a ball curves, it is the displacement in the *y* direction that we mean.

Given the horizontal speed of the pitch and the horizontal force on the ball, we can use the equation above to compute how far a ball will

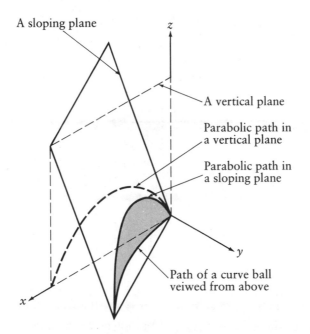

A sloping plane

z

A vertical plane

Parabolic path in a vertical plane

Parabolic path in a sloping plane

y

Path of a curve ball veiwed from above

x

FIGURE 11. *Most curve balls are thrown in such a way that the balls experience both a sideward force and a downward force (in addition to the force of gravity). A viewer directly above the pitcher and without depth perception would see the horizontal motion of the ball in the xy plane as a parabolic arc in which the ball curves to the side.*

curve horizontally. A baseball weighs about 5.2 ounces. Suppose a horizontal force just half this large, 2.6 ounces, could be imposed on the ball. If the horizontal speed of the ball is 80 miles per hour (118 feet per second), the time to reach home plate is (from equation $x = v_{x0}t$) 0.512 second, and, by the equation above, the ball will curve horizontally by $y = \frac{1}{2}(\frac{1}{2})(32)(0.512)^2 = 2.1$ feet. (The vertical distance that the pitch would drop due to its weight is $z = \frac{1}{2}(32)(0.512)^2 = 4.19$ feet.) This would, of course, be quite a good pitch. In Chapter 3 we will see whether it is possible to impose a 2.6 ounce horizontal force on a baseball. Before going on to describe and discuss the forces that can cause a ball to curve, it will be instructive to take one final look at the formulae we have been using.

The time it takes for a ball to go a horizontal distance x is given by the equation

$$t = \frac{x}{v_{x0}}$$

If we substitute this value of t into

$$y = \frac{1}{2}\left[\frac{F_y g}{w}\right] t^2$$

we find the following expression for the distance the ball curves.

$$y = \frac{1}{2}\left[\frac{F_y}{w}\right] g \left[\frac{x}{v_{x0}}\right]^2$$

The form of this equation tells us much about the motion of a curving baseball. First of all, the distance y that the ball curves depends inversely on the mass of the ball: $m = w/g$. (As long as we confine our discussion to objects near the surface of the Earth, where g does not vary much, we can think of mass as reflecting the weight of the object.) A ball that is half as massive, that is, "heavy," as a baseball will curve twice as far; a ball that is twice as massive will curve only half as far. Ping-Pong balls, whiffle balls, tennis balls, and the like can curve a lot even when subjected to small forces. This inverse relationship between the distance a ball curves and its mass is what prompted the author of the 1941 *Life* magazine article[8] to write that "it is perfectly true that a person can put a curve on a ping-pong ball or a tennis ball . . . but a baseball is so heavy an object for its size in comparison to a tennis ball or ping-pong ball that the pitcher's spinning action appears to be insufficient to change its course." We shall see.

Finally, the form of the equation just given can be used to shed light on the controversy about whether a curve ball breaks or curves smoothly. One popular explanation of the perceived break of a curve ball attributes it to an optical illusion. Imagine yourself standing by the side of a railroad track watching an oncoming train. To quote directly from an article in *Life* magazine (1952)[9]: "A railroad train seems to go faster and faster as it gets nearer a watcher until it appears to 'break' to the side with a great whoosh and whip by, causing the onlooker to duck—although the train's course and speed is constant. A batter is subjected to the same visual magnifications as he watches a ball speed towards him." But then why doesn't a straight ball appear to break? Clearly, this is not an adequate explanation. Let's look in a little more detail at the flight of a curve ball.

According to the above equation, a ball subjected to a constant horizontal force curves in a smooth arc, but let us examine this arc more closely. Recall that we computed that an 80-mile-an-hour curve ball subjected to a horizontal force of 2.6 ounces would curve by 2.1 feet on its way to home plate. We could also obtain this directly from the equation above, where we show y as a function of distance:

$$y(60) = \frac{1}{2} \left[\frac{2.6}{5.2} \right] (32) \left[\frac{60}{118} \right]^2 = 2.1 \text{ ft}$$

However, during the first half of its flight, it curves only

$$y(30) = \frac{1}{2} \left[\frac{2.6}{5.2} \right] (32) \left[\frac{30}{118} \right]^2 = 0.52 \text{ ft}$$

This means it has to curve 1.58 feet during the last half of its flight, 3 times as far as it does during the first half. In fact, half of the total 2.1 feet that the ball moves in the y direction occurs during the last 17.6 feet of its flight toward home plate.

It is even more impressive to look at these figures in another way. During the first 10 feet the ball moves

$$y(10) = \frac{1}{2} \left[\frac{2.6}{5.2} \right] (32) \left[\frac{10}{118} \right]^2 = 0.058 \text{ ft}$$

in the y direction (less than three quarters of an inch). During the first 50 feet, it moves

$$y(50) = \frac{1}{2} \left[\frac{2.6}{5.2} \right] (32) \left[\frac{50}{118} \right]^2 = 1.45 \text{ ft}$$

in the y direction. Therefore it curves by $2.1 - 1.45 = 0.65$ feet (nearly eight inches) during the *last* 10 feet. The ball moves laterally more than 10 times further during the *last* 10 feet of the trip to the plate than it moves laterally during the *first* 10 feet. The ball isn't simply drifting away from its initial direction along the x-axis — it is *accelerating* away from the hitter. The parabolic arc* is smooth, but the break is no optical illusion.

In this chapter we showed that if a horizontal force could be put on a baseball, then the ball would follow a parabolic arc, that is, a curve. In the next chapter we will explain where these forces come from. Then, in Chapter 4, we will describe several scientific experiments that were conducted to measure the horizontal forces on baseballs. The results of these experiments, together with the equations developed in this chapter, can then be used to calculate the deflections actually experienced by curve balls, knuckleballs, and other pitches.

Notes

1. W. F. Allman, "Pitching Rainbows," *Science82*, October 1982, pp. 32–39.

2. C. Einstein, *The Fireside Book of Baseball*, Simon and Schuster, New York, 1987, p. 99.

3. R. W. Madden, Letter to the editor, *The New Yorker*, May 24, 1941, pp. 53–54.

4. N. Houston, Letter to the editor, *The New Yorker*, July 5, 1941, p. 44.

5. L. Stanton, Letter to the editor, *The New Yorker*, June 7, 1941, p. 70.

6. R. Smith, *Baseball*, Simon & Schuster, 1947, p. 73.

7. R. D. Lillibridge, Letter to the editor, *The New Yorker*, June 7, 1941, p. 69.

8. Anonymous, "Baseball's Curve Balls: Are They Optical Illusions," *Life*, September 15, 1941, p. 83–89.

9. Anonymous, "Camera and science settle the old rhubarb about baseball's curveball," *Life*, July 27, 1953, pp. 104–107.

*Actually, the force is always perpendicular to the direction of motion of the ball, as we will see in Chapters 3 and 4. The motion of the ball under a force perpendicular to its motion is a circular arc.

The Origin of Forces on a Baseball

The fact that tennis balls curve because of the spin imparted to them was noted as early as 1671 by Sir Isaac Newton.[1] In 1877 the English Scientist Lord Rayleigh,[2] in a paper also describing the irregular flight of the tennis ball, credited the German engineer G. Magnus with the first explanation of the lateral deflection of a spinning ball. This phenomenon, in fact, derives its name from its explicator: *the Magnus effect.* Magnus's explanation, however, was published in 1853 (according to Barkla and Auchterlonie[3]), more than a century after a similar explanation had been given by Robins[4] in *New Principles of Gunnery.* Both Magnus and Robins were interested in the trajectories of cannonballs and of musket balls. Robins experimented with the effects of spin on the curvature of the paths of musket balls by firing them from a gun with a slightly curved barrel. With the barrel bent to the left, the ball was forced into contact with the right side of the bore, thus imparting spin on the ball in the clockwise direction when viewed from above. The paths of the musket balls fired in this way were curved to the right.

The explanation given by Robins and Magnus went as follows: a spinning musket ball creates a whirlpool of air around it in addition to the linear flow of the air past the ball due to its motion through space. This circulating air slows down the flow of air past the ball on the left side and speeds it up on the right side. A theorem of Daniel Bernoulli, an eighteenth-century Swiss mathematician, states that when the speed of a fluid (like air) increases, its pressure decreases. (See box, pages 42 and 43.) Thus, the left side of the ball, where the air speed is slower, experiences a higher pressure than the right side. The resulting pressure (and force) imbalance caused the ball to move laterally toward the right side.

What really happens is a bit more complicated than this. It involves a thin layer of fluid very close to the solid wall of the sphere called the *boundary layer*. Because every fluid possesses *viscosity*, there is a shearing force between adjacent regions of the fluid that move at different speeds. By rubbing your hands against each other or pushing a book across a table top you can experience a shearing force. Let's see how shearing forces affect a fluid in motion.

Imagine a fluid flowing past a flat wall, and imagine that the fluid consists of many layers of molecules, one layer next to the other. Experiments have shown that the fluid layer immediately adjacent to the wall essentially "sticks" to the wall. Every other layer rubs against layers adjacent to it, resulting in shearing forces between the layers. Through these shearing forces, the faster-moving layers drag the slower layers along. The fluid far from the wall is practically unaffected by the presence of the wall. It moves at what we call the *free stream velocity*. The layer adjacent to the wall is *totally* affected by the presence of the wall in the sense that it "sticks" to the wall. There is a region between these extremes where the shearing force caused by the viscosity of the fluid is of great importance. This region, where the layers of fluid rub against one another to create a shearing force, is called the *boundary layer*, because it is present near solid boundaries. It is, of course, a group of layers in the sense that we have been using the term *layer*. Figure 12 is a drawing of motion in a boundary layer near a wall. Here the fluid is water. A pulse of electricity was sent through a tiny wire, the vertical line on the left side of the drawing, causing a chemical reaction that produced a colored line in the water. A photograph was taken a moment later. You can see that the colored water near the wall moved more slowly than that farther from the wall, indicating that the speed of the water decreased from the free stream value far from the wall to zero at the wall. The same phenomenon occurs when air flows past a baseball (or, equivalently, when a baseball moves through air). The thickness of the boundary layer in that case is very small — only a millimeter or two. Yet its presence is crucial to the ability of a pitcher to manipulate the paths of his pitches. Let us now see why.

If the viscosity of the air were zero, the air would flow around the ball as shown in Figure 13. Think of a small piece of fluid, called a *fluid particle*, within the fluid as a whole. As a fluid particle at point A in the figure approaches the ball and begins to move around it, from the front

Bernoulli's Principle

Bernoulli's principle states that regions of higher velocity in a fluid correspond to regions of lower pressure. This principle is actually a direct result of Newton's second law. To see this consider what happens when a constant force F is applied to a mass m. The mass will accelerate and will attain a form of energy called *kinetic energy*. This energy results directly from *work* done on the mass by the force. The work done by a constant force is defined as the force multiplied by the distance through which it moves. According to Newton's second law, the work W is

$$W = F \cdot d = m \cdot a \cdot d$$

Now suppose the mass initially has zero speed. Then after a time t it will attain a certain speed v. The acceleration is v/t and the distance the mass moves is the average speed multiplied by t or $d = v_{avg}t = \frac{1}{2}vt$. The work can now be expressed as

$$W = m \left(\frac{v}{t}\right)\left(\frac{1}{2}vt\right) = \frac{1}{2}mv^2$$

The quantity $\frac{1}{2}mv^2$ is the kinetic energy.

Now consider the case of a fluid in motion. A line within the fluid to which the velocity vector is tangent is called a *streamline*. If the flow is steady, the fluid always moves along the streamlines. We then imagine a tube made of up streamlines. Since the flow is always tangent to the streamlines, the tube behaves as though it were a real tube in the sense that fluid flows through it without leaking from the sides. Such a stream tube is shown here.

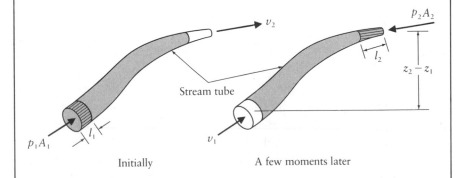

Initially   A few moments later

At a certain time a certain identifiable portion of fluid occupies the shaded portion of the tube as shown in the left part of the figure. A moment later this fluid has moved to a new portion of the tube as shown on the right. The

Bernoulli's Principle (*continued*)

motion was caused by pressure forces. How much work has been done in moving the shaded portion of the fluid from the first position to the second position? The fluid within the large central portion of the streamline has undergone no change. It is as though the portion of fluid of volume $A_1 l_1$ located at the bottom left, the inlet of the stream tube, suddenly appeared at the upper right, the exit of the stream tube.

As long as no fluid is stored within the stream tube, the mass of fluid entering must be the same as that leaving. Using the symbol ρ to denote density (mass per volume), the mass entering or leaving is

$$\rho A_1 l_1 = \rho A_2 l_2$$

Work is done on the fluid by the pressure force $p_1 A_1$ in the amount $p_1 A_1 l$. Work is done at the exit of the stream tube in the amount $- p_2 A_2 l_2$. Note that this quantity is negative because the directions of the force $p_2 A_2$ and the distance moved l_2 are opposite. Instead of work being done *on* the fluid, work has been done *by* the fluid. Work has also been done *against* the force of gravity in lifting the fluid. The gravitational force is the mass of the fluid times the gravitational acceleration, and so the work done by gravity is $- \rho A_1 l_1 g$ $(z_2 - z_2)$. The kinetic energy increase caused by the work is the difference between $\frac{1}{2} m v^2$ of the portion leaving the tube and that entering the tube:

$$p_1 A_1 l_1 - p_2 A_2 l_2 - \rho A_1 l_1 g \, (z_2 - z_1) = \frac{1}{2} \, \rho A_1 l_1 \left(v_2^2 - v_1^2 \right)$$

If the density is constant, the volume flowing into the tube is the same as that flowing out, so that $A_1 l_1 = A_2 l_2$. In this case the above equation can be divided by $\rho A_1 l_1$ resulting in Bernoulli's equation

$$\frac{p_1}{\rho} + g z_1 + \frac{v_1^2}{2} = \frac{p_2}{\rho} + g z_2 + \frac{v_2^2}{2}$$

For the situations we will be studying (air at fairly high speeds flowing past baseballs) $g z_1$ is very nearly equal to $g z_2$ and these two terms may be safely neglected. Furthermore, since positions 1 and 2 are arbitrary, $p/\rho + v^2/2$ must be the same everywhere along the streamline. Finally, we note that Bernoulli's equation is true when $v = 0$. Hence, one can theoretically always follow a streamline to a place where $v = 0$ and then switch to another streamline. We conclude that $p/\rho + v^2/2 + gz$ is constant throughout the fluid. Hence, if the speed, and therefore the kinetic energy, increases the pressure must decrease so that the sum of the pressure and kinetic energy remains constant.

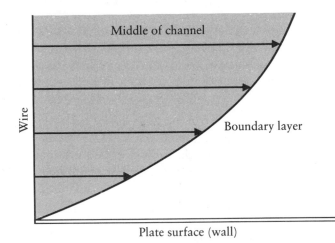

Middle of channel

Wire

Boundary layer

Plate surface (wall)

FIGURE 12. *The behavior of a fluid flowing from left to right in a flat channel. At the bottom is the wall of a channel. The top of the drawing is the middle of the channel. The arrows pointing to the dark edge show how far the particles have gone since the dye was released. Particles far from the wall have moved with the free stream velocity, while particles closer to the wall (within the boundary layer) have moved more slowly.*

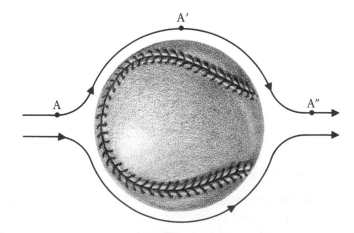

A′

A   A″

FIGURE 13. *The flow of an* ideal *fluid having no viscosity. The speed of the fluid increases as it goes from point A to point A′ and then decreases as it goes from point A′ to A″. As the speed increases, the pressure of the fluid decreases because a pressure force is required to accelerate the fluid. The pressure decreases between points A′ and A″ because a negative force is required to slow the fluid down. There is no net force on the sphere in this ideal situation because the pressure forces on the top and the bottom and on the front and back cancel each other.*

(at *A*) toward the equator at *A'*), it will accelerate. This means that its speed, and therefore its kinetic energy, or energy of motion, will increase. (See box, page 42.) In order for this to happen, the fluid particle must have had a force pushing on it. The force that causes the fluid particle to accelerate comes from a pressure difference between points *A* and *A'*. According to Bernoulli's principle, the pressure in the fluid at *A* is greater than the pressure at *A'*. Thus, in going from point *A* to point *A'*, the kinetic energy of the fluid particle increases as a result of work done on the fluid particle by pressure force. Now imagine the same fluid particle as it goes from point *A'* to point *A''* near the rear of the ball. Again, because of Bernoulli's principle, exactly the reverse of what we have described above happens. The pressure at point *A'* is smaller than at *A''*; the fluid particle is slowed down, and the kinetic energy that was gained through work done by the pressure force between *A* and *A'* is given back to the rising pressure between *A'* and *A''*.

To understand the effect of shearing forces in the fluid flow past a ball, we first consider an easier example. Imagine yourself pushing a block across a frictionless table from *A* to *A'* as in Figure 14. As you push the block its speed increases as a result of the work you do on the block. The pressure of your finger against the block is similar to the pressure of the fluid on the fluid particle in Figure 13. Now reverse the procedure as the block moves from *A'* to *A''*. As you push against the block in the opposite direction from its motion, the block slows down again. (You have actually done negative work, because the block has done work on you!)

Now imagine yourself going through the same procedure with the block on a table that is *not* frictionless. Refer to Figure 15. This time, as

FIGURE 14. *The reversible nature of the force–acceleration interaction in the absence of friction. The block is initially stationary at point A. If we push the block along a frictionless table, it accelerates and reaches a certain speed at point A'. If we now reverse the force, the block decelerates until it comes to rest at point A''.*

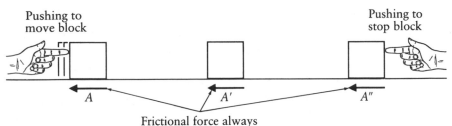

Pushing to
move block

Pushing to
stop block

A

A'

A''

Frictional force always
opposes motion

FIGURE 15. *If friction is present and the force profile of Figure 14 is used, the block will not reach point A", because frictional forces always oppose motion. When a force toward the right is imposed at point A, the block accelerates towards point A'. Because of the frictional force, however, its speed will be lower than that of the block in Figure 14. When the negative, braking force is now imposed on the block, it is aided by the frictional force. The deceleration is faster, and the block comes to rest to the left of point A". If the force continues to be imposed, the block actually reverses direction.*

you do work on the block to speed it up, you must work against a frictional force that wants to slow the block down. Still, you push hard enough to get the block up to a certain speed at A'. When you reverse the process after passing A', the frictional force is *helping* you to slow the block down. The block will, of course, stop before it comes to point A''. It will, in fact, reverse directions if you keep pushing.

Finally, imagine the (real) flow of air past a baseball with (viscous) frictional force included. Refer to Figure 16. The fluid particles in the boundary layer will behave similarly to the block on the frictional table in our thought experiment above. As a fluid particle in the boundary layer moves past point A' at the equator, it slows down. Of course, the free stream flow finally sweeps the fluid particle downstream. On the downstream side of the ball, however, the fluid particle stops before reaching the rearward pole. (See box, page 47.) A region called the *wake region* develops, where the air experiences a swirling, chaotic flow. You are probably familiar with wakes behind boats. You can also see this phenomenon on the downstream sides of bridge abutments. We call the point on the surface where the wake begins the *separation point*, and the phenomenon itself *boundary layer separation*.

Because of the chaotic flow, the pressure in the wake region is significantly lower than the pressure on the front of the ball. This is because the kinetic energy lost by the fluid particles in traveling from the equator to downstream is bound up in the turbulent eddies in the wake

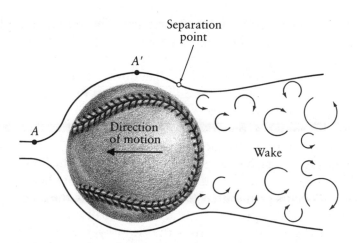

FIGURE 16. *The flow of a real fluid (like air) around a ball. Since the fluid possesses viscosity, fluid particles in the boundary layer stop before going all the way around the ball. At some point beyond A′ a region of backflow develops. The flow in the free stream ultimately pushes the fluid past the ball, but the development of the backflow near the ball produces a region of chaotic, swirling flow around the rear of the ball. This region is called the wake, and the point where it begins is called the separation point.*

Bernoulli Equation with Loss

In a real fluid another work term must be added to the analysis from which the Bernoulli equation was derived. This is the work done by a fluid particle in order to overcome viscous or frictional forces that are always present in any real fluid. Frictional forces do work to impede motion. Thus, the frictional term will serve to decrease the speed v_2 of the fluid at the end of the stream tube (as seen in the box on page 42) below the value predicted in that box. The Bernoulli equation *with losses* is

$$\frac{p_1}{\rho} + \frac{v_1^2}{2} + gz_1 = \frac{p_2}{\rho} + \frac{v_2^2}{2} + gz_2 + L$$

in which L is a positive quantity.

instead of being added back to the pressure. The existence of the wake creates a drag force. If the wake is symmetrical (which occurs when the ball is not spinning and when there are no irregularities on the ball's surface) the drag will simply slow the ball down. If, however, the wake is not symmetrical, it will have the additional effect of redirecting the flow coming off the rear of the ball.

Figure 17 shows a remarkable photograph of the flow around a spinning baseball taken by the late Professor F. N. M. Brown of Notre Dame University. The ball is spinning clockwise and the flow of the air is from left to right. Separation is delayed (occurs further back) on the top surface and occurs prematurely (further forward) on the bottom surface. Put rather simplistically, if the surface of the ball moves along with the flow, less energy is drained from the flow by the shearing forces of viscosity, and the separation is delayed—as happens with the top surface. If the surface of the ball moves opposite to the flow, the frictional effects are enhanced, and separation occurs earlier—as happens with the bottom surface. The shifted wake region has the effect of deflecting the flow of air downward as it passes the ball. This has the same effect on the ball that a rudder has on a boat. If, as a boat moves through the water, the rudder is placed so that it deflects water toward the right, the rear of the boat is forced toward the left. The baseball in Figure 17 will be forced upward as the airflow is deflected downward. Clearly, by throwing a baseball with spin about one axis or another, a pitcher can cause the ball to curve to the right or to the left, or to rise above or fall below its normal parabolic arc.

If the ball has backspin, for example, it will rise above its normal parabolic arc, like a rising fastball. If the ball has top spin it will drop. If it spins around a vertical axis like a top, it will move horizontally. Usually the axis of rotation is inclined. For example, a right-handed pitcher sees the curve ball leave his hand with its axis of rotation pointed to the upper left so that it has both top spin and a counterclockwise rotation (when viewed from above). This makes the ball drop (because of the top spin) and curve away from a right-handed batter (because of the counterclockwise rotation). A right-handed pitcher would see his screwball leave with its axis of rotation pointed to the upper right so that it has both top spin and a clockwise rotation. This ball drops and curves toward a right-handed batter (because of the clockwise rotation). The orientation of the axis of rotation depends on the pitcher's arm, wrist, and finger actions during the delivery. For example, a fastball thrown with a straight overhand delivery will not curve to the side, whereas the same pitch thrown with a three-quarter overhand delivery

FIGURE 17. *A ball rotating in a wind tunnel. The ball is spinning clockwise and the air is flowing left to right. The paths of fluid particles of air are made visible by introducing streamers of smoke into the air. Since the upper surface of the ball moves in the same direction as the free stream flow, the air flows further around the ball before separation occurs. Conversely, the motion of the bottom surface of the ball is opposed to the flow, and separation occurs sooner. Because of the off-center wake, the flow of air past the ball is deflected downward in this case. The downward force required to deflect the wake must be balanced by an equal and opposite upward force on the ball by the air. [Photograph F. N. M. Brown, University of Notre Dame; courtesy, Thomas J. Mueller]*

will have some curve. Therefore, the direction of movement depends on the orientation of the spin axis. The amount of movement depends on the speed and the rotation rate of the pitch.

Table 1 shows typical values of these two parameters for a wide variety of pitches and pitchers. We do not use all the information in this table now, but we will repeatedly refer to it. These are "ball park figures," not scientific data; they represent the melding of data from many sources. Of course, there are people whose abilities lie outside of these ranges, but they are atypical. The top five entries are for major-league pitchers. Speed refers to speed when the ball leaves the pitcher's hand, in miles per hour. Spin rate refers to the estimated spin rate in revolutions per minute; the range, for the top four lines, is about ± 300 rpm. Rotations refers to the number of times the ball turns around on its trip from the pitcher to the plate.

We have not discussed the pitcher's grip on the ball. The grip makes the difference between the rising fastball, the sinking fastball, the split-fingered fastball, the fork ball, the knuckle ball, and the change-up, according to Kindall.[5] These pitches are all thrown with about the same

TABLE 1 Typical Characteristics of Various Pitches			
Type of Pitch	Speed (mph)	Typical Spin Rate (rpm)	Rotations Enroute to Plate
Fastball	85 to 95	1600	11
Slider	75 to 85	1700	13
Curve ball	70 to 80	1900	16
Change-up	60 to 70	1500	14
Knuckle ball	60 to 70	25 to 50	$1/4$ to $1/2$
Typical fathers	40 to 50		
7- to 9-year-old boys	30 to 40		

arm motion, but the different grips produce different speeds, rotation rates, and axes of rotation. These three parameters in turn change the trajectories of the balls. In this book we discuss these three parameters and not the grip on the ball.

Besides putting spin on the ball, there are other ways of manipulating the wake — some legal and some illegal. Pitches like knuckle balls, spitballs, and scuff balls are other examples of pitches in which the pitcher manipulates the wake to produce a lateral force on the ball. Let's see how this manipulation is accomplished.

The German aerodynamicist C. Weisselsberger discovered early in this century that by placing a wire around the front part of a smooth sphere one could, under certain conditions, delay boundary layer separation and the formation of the wake (Figure 18). The wire apparently introduces turbulence into the boundary layer near the sphere, increasing its communication with the fluid further away from the surface, so that it can be swept further around the sphere. In other words, the shearing force between outer layers of the fluid is increased.

Because of the presence of its seams, a *nonspinning* baseball offers to an airstream a nonsymmetrical version of this picture. On one side of the baseball the presence of stitches or seams may delay separation, while on the other side they may not. Figure 19 is a sketch showing what happens. With the seams in the position shown, the top part of the ball is smooth, but the seam region on the bottom causes the boundary layer to become turbulent, delaying separation. The wake shifts upward, redirecting air flow in that direction and forcing the ball downward.

FIGURE 18. *The point where separation occurs and the wake forms can be manipulated by altering the surface of the sphere. (Permission of Office National d' Études et de Recherches Aérospatiales).*

Note that once again, as for the curve ball, it is the shifted wake that leads to the lateral force on the ball.

One reason the knuckle ball is so notoriously difficult to hit is that there are an infinite number of ways to orient the seams. Each will cause a different force. No two pitches will behave in exactly the same way. Many people think that a knuckle ball is a spinless pitch. Knuckle ball pitchers know, however, that a good knuckle ball is thrown so that it spins very slowly and makes perhaps one half a revolution on the way to home plate. As the locations of the seams relative to the air flow change, the position of the wake actually moves around, so the ball is forced first one way and then another. This explains the erratic paths of these pitches.

The knuckle ball is normally thrown by holding the ball with the first knuckles of one or more fingers, rather than with the fingertips. As the ball is released, the fingers are extended, inhibiting the normal backspin of the ball.

There are a number of other ways to throw a baseball so that it has very little spin. One method is to make the fingers slippery by applying

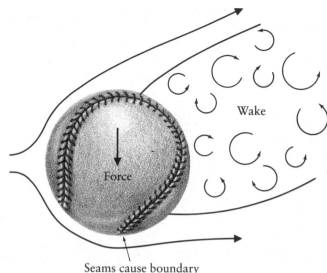

Seams cause boundary
layer turbulence

FIGURE 19. *The flow around a spinless ball. The ball is oriented in such a way that the top is smooth, while the stitches along the bottom surface act in much the same way as the wire in Figure 18. Separation is thus delayed on the lower surface and the resulting upward deflection of the wake causes a downward force on the ball.*

some foreign material like petroleum jelly or saliva to the fingertips, but not to the thumb. (Many of the old-timers chewed a substance called slippery elm for this purpose.) In releasing the ball, the pitcher squeezes it out between his fingers and thumb the way one would squeeze a watermelon seed, thus inhibiting backspin. As mentioned in Chapter 1, the knuckle ball became common a few years after the spitball was outlawed. It was, in fact, first known as the dry spitter. It is interesting to note that the spitball was outlawed because it was said to be too difficult to control and therefore dangerous to hitters. According to Ray Miller, the spitball is, in fact, easier to control than is the knuckle ball. There is other evidence that this is true. Many baseball insiders say that more major-league pitchers commonly throw spitballs than knuckle balls.

Another illegal pitch owing its behavior to shifting wake is the scuff ball or emery ball. The ball is prepared by scuffing it on one spot so that one side is much rougher than the other. The ball is then thrown so that the rough spot remains on one side. The rough spot delays boundary layer separation on that side, shifting the wake, and causing the ball to curve toward the roughened spot.

In this chapter we have explained the lateral movement of a baseball in terms of altering the wake behind it. Using the analogy of a boat in water, we explained that pushing the tiller to the left moves the rudder to the right. This deflects the water (the wake) to the right, which pushes the rear of the boat to the left and turns the boat to the right. We showed two quite different mechanisms that could move the wake of a baseball. the first explains why a curve ball curves. The rotation of the curve ball delays the separation on one side and advances the separation point on the other, thus producing an off-center wake and, therefore, lateral motion of the ball. The second mechanism for moving the wake explained the movement of the knuckle ball and scuff ball. A rough surface on one side of a nonspinning ball will delay the separation point and alter the wake, again producing a lateral force.

Now that we have seen how forces can be imposed on spinning and nonspinning balls, we turn to other questions. How large are these forces? How far can these forces make a ball curve? These are the topics of the next chapter.

Notes

1. I. Newton, "A Letter of Mr. Isaac Newton, of the University of Cambridge, Containing His New Theory About Light and Colors," *Philos. Trans. R. Soc.* Vol. 7, 1671–72, 3075–3087.

2. Lord Rayleigh, "On the Irregular Flight of a Tennis-Ball," *Messenger of Math*, Vol. 7, 1877–78, pp. 14–16.

3. H. Barkla and L. Auchterlonie, "The Magnus or Robins Effect on Rotating Spheres," *J. Fluid Mech.* Vol. 47, 1971, 437–447.

4. B. Robins, *New Principles of Gunnery*, Hutton, London, 1742.

5. J. Kindall, *Sports Illustrated Baseball*, Harper & Row, New York, 1983.

The Flight of the Ball:
Forces on Curve Balls and
Other Pitches

ince the photographic investigation published in 1941 by *Life* magazine, a number of articles have appeared in scientific journals and popular magazines seeking to answer definitively the question of whether a baseball curves—and whether it curves smoothly or "breaks." In April, 1942, less than a year after the appearance of the *Life* magazine article, a note appeared in the *American Journal of Physics* describing an experimental study by Verwiebe[1] that was almost identical to the fictional one performed by Rick Rover. Five wooden frames with nets of fine cotton thread (rather than the wet tissue paper "used" in the Rover Boys experiment) were placed between the pitcher's mound and home plate. "Straight balls," "right-

handed outdrops," and "left-handed outdrops" were thrown through
the frames by pitchers on a college baseball team. The "outdrops"
curved in the horizontal plane by 2.5 to 6.5 inches. The curve was
reported to be smooth, with no sharp "break" observed. An interesting
observation reported by Verwiebe[1] was that the balls also "dropped
more sharply than would be the case for free fall alone." We will have
more to say about this feature of the curve ball later.

On the June 19, 1949, *Look* magazine published "Visual Proof That a
Baseball Curves," and on July 27, 1953, *Life* magazine, this time using
Gjon Mili's strobe photography of pitches thrown by Ken Raffensberger
of the Cincinnati Reds, reversed itself, claiming that the curve ball
curves but does not "break." Some interesting new data came out of the
photographic study. By painting one half of the baseball black, the
investigators made it easy to see from the photographs how rapidly the
baseball was rotating. The Raffensberger curve rotated at about 1400
revolutions per minute (rpm) and had a speed of 43 miles per hour
(mph), which is very slow. (See Table 1.) Joseph Bicknell, a professor of
aeronautical engineering at MIT, reportedly determined, using a wind
tunnel test, that such a pitch should curve by approximately 6 inches.

In the summer of 1982, *Science82* magazine, together with the three
scientists, Robert Watts of Tulane University, Jim Walton of General
Motors, and Charlie Miller of MIT, set out to produce and study
high-speed stroboscopic photographs of baseballs pitched by Scott
McGregor, a pitcher for the Baltimore Orioles, and by Ray Miller, the
Orioles's pitching coach. Watts and Walton[2] reported in an address to
the American Association for the Advancement of Science that McGregor's curve balls did indeed curve, the total deflections being somewhat
less than 1 foot.

These are not very impressive numbers. Any baseball player would
reject them as being too small. Considerably more impressive numbers
have, in fact, been reported. Watts and Walton[2] reported that curve
balls propelled by a pitching machine curved by about 2 feet. Selin[3]
photographed and analyzed pitches thrown by college players in the Big
Ten Conference and concluded that curve balls thrown by these
pitchers suffered deflections of 0.4 to 2.2 feet. The speeds of these
pitches were reported to range between 50 and 76 mph, while the balls
rotated at 1150 to 2310 rpm.

Other wind tunnel tests (in addition to the one performed by Bicknell
and referred to in the 1953 *Life* magazine article) have also been performed. Briggs[4] reported that an 80 mph curve ball spinning at 1800 rpm
could curve as much as 17.5 inches, and Igor Sikorsky, a famous aerody-

SIMPLE CURVE

COMPOUND CURVE

REVERSED CURVE

namicist, is reported by Drury[5] to have found that a baseball rotating at only 600 rpm and with a horizontal speed of 80 mph would curve by up to 19 inches.

In view of the differences in the deflections of curve balls reported by different writers, it might prove both interesting and useful to examine the original sources a bit more closely in order to see whether the different results are really at odds with one another, or whether there is a way to reconcile them.

We begin by pointing out that many people think of a curve ball curving only horizontally, and we have perhaps served to perpetuate that myth through our example involving a horizontal force at the end of Chapter 2. What Verwiebe[1] measured, for example, were the horizontal deflections of what he referred to as "right-handed and left-handed outdrops." The fact that the vertical deviation of a curve ball from its otherwise parabolic trajectory is often larger than its horizontal deflection is well-known to those who play baseball professionally, and even to many serious amateurs. In fact, one customarily sees and hears a word like "outdrop" when pitchers describe their pitches. We might recall that the 1941 *Life* magazine article referred to Cy Blanton's curve ball as being "a straight ball with a decided drop," and that Verwiebe observed in his 1942 experiment that the right-handed and left-handed outdrops "dropped more sharply than would be the case for free fall alone." Ray Miller pointed out that this is by design, not by accident. In his 1981 article, Bill Allman[6] reported:

> "The Ball has to break down," says Ray Miller, pitching coach for the Baltimore Orioles, "or it's not an effective pitch. The hitting area of the bat is three inches wide and eight inches long. A ball that breaks horizontally is just going to hit another part of the bat."

A baseball bat is essentially a cylindrical piece of wood that is used to strike the pitched ball. It is generally swung in such a way that the axis of the cylinder is approximately parallel to the ground (that is, approximately horizontal). An error in the horizontal position of the bat is therefore nowhere near as serious as an error in its vertical position. Missing by an inch or two horizontally is often not terribly serious, but an error of a fraction of an inch in the bat's vertical position can mean the difference between a line drive and a pop-up. As Kirkpatrick[7] rather humorously pointed out, "The 1962 world championship was finally determined by an otherwise perfect swing of a bat which came to the collision 1 mm too high to effect the transfer of title." We will suggest in the last section of Chapter 5 that the error was probably larger than this. However, the argument that the margin for error is greater horizontally than vertically remains true.

The forces that give rise to the "outdrop" have the same origin as the forces on the curve ball that we described in Chapter 3. They are caused by the spin of the ball. The direction of the force on a moving, spinning ball is determined by the relative directions of the ball speed (or the opposite of the air flowing past the ball) and the axis of rotation of the ball. In fact, the lateral (curving) force is in a direction mutually perpendicular to the direction in which the ball is traveling and to the direction of the axis of rotation. If the pitcher throws a sidearm curve, he can probably make the axis of rotation of the ball nearly vertical, so that the lateral forces will be horizontal. Generally, pitchers throw with a motion somewhere between directly overarm and sidearm. The result is that the axis of rotation is not vertical. Figure 20 shows the result. The lateral force is not horizontal, and can be represented (remember the discussion of Figure 2) as two forces F_y (horizontal) and F_z (vertical).

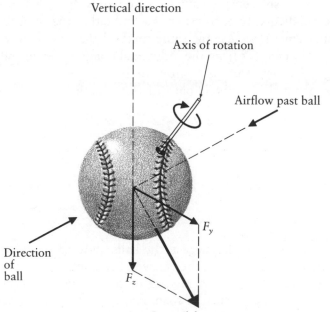

FIGURE 20. *The force on a rotating ball is mutually perpendicular to the axis of rotation and the direction of air flow past the ball.*

Since Verwiebe did not give quantitative information about the "drop" part of his "outdrops," it is impossible to tell just how much the curve balls of his experiments were deflected from the parabolic path caused by gravity alone acting on the balls. Suppose, however, that the pitcher is able to cause a force F_y to act horizontally on the ball and, in addition, to cause a force of F_z to act downward on the ball. In a sense, the ball would then have an apparent weight of $w + F_z$. The weight of the ball causes it to fall through a distance $z_2 = 1/2 \, gt^2$. The extra downward force causes the ball to drop by an additional distance

$$z_3 = \frac{F_z g t^2}{2w}$$

This derivation is similar to that of the equation

$$y = 1/2 \left[\frac{F_y g}{w}\right] t^2$$

which is the expression of horizontal displacement due to a force F_y. The two displacement values caused only by the forces F_y and F_z are perpendicular to each other. To find either the total force or the total displacement, we use the same method that we used to calculate the speed v in Figure 7 from the individual components v_y and v_z. Thus, the nongravitational force acting on the ball is $F = \sqrt{F_y^2 + F_z^2}$, and the deflection from the parabolic path of the equation

$$z = v_{z_0} t - 1/2 \, gt^2$$

is

$$d = \sqrt{z_3^2 + y^2} = \frac{F g t^2}{2w}$$

If, as Ray Miller's remarks suggest, the balls photographed by Verwiebe curved downward more than they curved horizontally, the z_3 could be a good deal larger than y. In any case, the values he measured and reported were certainly smaller than the real deflection of the curve.

What about Scott McGregor's curve ball? The deflection of McGregor's curve ball of somewhat less than 1 foot as reported by Watts and Walton was the *total deflection*; that is, both horizontal and vertical departures from the parabolic gravitational trajectory were considered. However, this experiment was flawed because the night before the photography session, McGregor had been called upon to pitch for the Orioles. Therefore, he was quite understandably throwing with some-what less than his maximum effort in the photographic session. The measured deflection cannot be expected to reflect those of a major league curve ball.

The 1953 *Life* magazine article reported that the "widest variance" of the Raffensberger curve ball "is in mid-flight . . . where it measured 6 inches." Elsewhere in the article, it is reported that "recreating as nearly as possible Raffensberger's pitch in a wind tunnel with an inge-nious gadget, Bicknell demonstrated that the ball was thrust sideways approximately six inches." The implication is that Bicknell measured the force on a baseball spinning at 1400 rpm in a wind tunnel with air speed set at 43 mph (the measured rotation and speed rate of Raffensberger's curve ball, respectively). He must then have computed the deflection of the ball using an equation like the equation

$$y = \frac{1}{2} \left[\frac{F_y g}{w}\right] t^2$$

Interestingly enough, his calculation seems to agree almost exactly with the "variance" of 6 inches actually measured. However, his 6-inch deflection and that reported by *Life* probably refer to different things. The one calculated by Bicknell refers, in all probability, to the displace-ment of the immediately preceding equation. The 6-inch "variance" of the Raffensberger curve ball most definitely does not, as we will now show.

The curved line in Figure 21 depicts the path of a curve ball as viewed directly from above, that is, in the *x-y* plane. (You may want to look back at the discussion of Figure 11 in Chapter 2.) The authors of the *Life* article joined "the beginning and the end of the curve's arc" with a straight line and measured the distance between the curve's arc and straight line at the midpoint. Some geometric distances are shown on the figure. The letter D is the distance the pitch travels in the x direction, y is the total deflection. Halfway along its path (at $D/2$) the straight line path would have moved over by $y/2$, but the parabolic curve would have moved only $y/(2)^2 = y/4$. The difference, $y/4$, represents the 6-inch measurement reported. Evidently, the horizontal deflection of the Raffensberger curve ball was an impressive $y = 4 \times 6$ inches $= 24$

FIGURE 21. *When* Life *magazine reported that a curve ball thrown by Ken Raffensberger curved by 6 inches, they were referring to widest variance between the path of the ball in midflight and a straight line connecting the initial and final positions of the baseball. In the text, we show that this is only one fourth of the actual deflection of the ball. The actual horizontal deflection of the ball, measured from the line it would have taken without the force caused by its spin, was an impressive 2 feet.*

inches! It is quite likely that Raffensberger threw a *sidearm curve,* a pitch that exaggerates the horizontal motion at the expense of the vertical motion, because he knew this was what the *Life* magazine people were going to measure. It is difficult to be sure why Bicknell reported a deflection of only 6 inches, because his measurement method was not reported in sufficient detail.

◆ Does the Amount of Curve Depend on Velocity
or Velocity Squared? ◆

The article by Drury[5] states that Sikorsky found that the deflection y of a spinning baseball on its path toward home plate is directly proportional to the rotation rate ω, the square of the velocity v of the ball, and the square of the time t required to reach home plate, and inversely proportional to the mass m of the ball:

$$y = \frac{K\,\omega v^2 t^2}{m}$$

Until recently, the most systematic experiment on the forces of spinning baseballs that is reported in useful detail in the scientific literature is one conducted by Briggs[4] of the National Bureau of Standards. The results of Briggs's tests indicate, as did the Sikorsky results, that the lateral force on the baseball is proportional to the rotation rate multiplied by the square of the velocity. However, these results conflict with a theorem in fluid mechanics called the Kutta-Zhukovskii theorem, which states that whenever a spinning two-dimensional object is moving through a fluid, and there is a net circulation of the fluid about the object, there results a force mutually perpendicular to the direction of the motion of the object and the direction of the axis of the spin. This force has a magnitude that is proportional to the product of the velocity and the rotation rate (ωv). Experimental measurements of lift on rotating cylinders appear to bear this out. It seems reasonable that the lift forces on a rotating sphere would also depend on ωv rather than ωv^2.

We have conducted a careful series of experiments designed to determine which of these is true.[8] The experimental arrangement that we used consisted of a subsonic wind tunnel, a device for measuring lift on a spinning ball, and devices for measuring the rotational and free stream velocities. Three baseballs were impaled on 6.3-mm-diameter shafts with the seams in the positions shown in Figure 22. The shaft of a particular ball was then mounted in a frame as shown in Figure 23. An impeller mounted on the end of the shaft was used for creating rotation by using a high-speed air jet issuing from a nozzle. The entire device was mounted in the test section of a subsonic wind tunnel. Air in the tunnel flows from right to left in Figure 23.

FIGURE 22. *In order to measure the forces on spinning baseballs, and to determine the effect of the orientation of the seams relative to the spin axis, we mounted three baseballs on thin shafts with three different seam orientations as shown in this figure, and studied them in a wind tunnel.*

FIGURE 23. *The baseballs in our experiment were mounted in the student laboratory wind tunnel at Tulane University as shown in this figure. Air from a nozzle was used to induce rotation and the wind tunnel forced air past the ball. The rotation rate was measured with a strobotachometer. Forces on the ball induced forces in Plexiglas supports. Strain gages in the supports were used to infer the forces on the spinning ball.*

Our measurements showed that the force on the baseball is proportional to ωv, not to ωv^2. The equation for the force on a spinning baseball that we obtained from our data is

$$F_L = 6.4 \times 10^{-7}\ \omega v$$

where F_L is in pounds, v is in feet per second, and ω is in revolutions per minute. Using this equation, we find that an 80-mph curve ball rotating at 2000 rpm would experience a lateral force of 0.15 lb, or 2.4 oz, which is just about what we said we needed back in Chapter 2. Figure 24 illustrates this equation graphically.

The reason we mounted the balls with three different seam orientations was to test whether this is an important factor in how far a curve ball curves. Many baseball players believe that it is an important factor, and that orientation 1 in Figure 22 would result in a better curve than

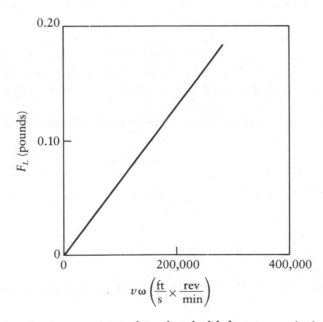

FIGURE 24. *Our measurements show that the lift force on a spinning baseball is almost linearly dependent on the product of the velocity and the rotation rate. While our measurements were limited to air speed values less than 40 miles per hour because of limitations of the wind tunnel, the use of dimensionless groups, as explained in the text, allows us to use data by other authors to infer that this is also true at higher air speeds.*

orientation 2 because orientation 1 puts "more strings into the wind." We found the orientation of the seams had virtually no effect on the force. Certain grips may, of course, allow the pitcher to get a higher rotation rate. As far as the force by the air on a rotating pitch is concerned, however, the positions of the seams are apparently of little significance. What is *very* important is the orientation of the *axis of rotation* of the ball. To maximize the curve, the axis of rotation should be precisely perpendicular to the direction of motion of the ball. Otherwise the lateral force caused by the rotation of the ball will decrease approximately as the sine of the angle between the axis of rotation and the direction of motion.

Both the time-honored Kutta-Zhukovskii theorem and the results of our experiments cast doubt on the velocity-squared results of Briggs and Sikorsky. Our measurements were performed in a wind tunnel in which the maximum speed of the air was about 40 miles per hour. Pitched baseballs travel as fast as 100 miles per hour. There comes the natural question, therefore, of whether our results are valid at speeds more than twice as large as those used in our experiments. Recent measurements of the forces on spinning golf balls by Bearman and Harvey[9] and by William Gobush (private communication) at high velocities also indicate that F_L depends on ωv, not ωv^2. In fact, if the difference in surface areas of the two types of balls is taken into account, the results of Bearman and Harvey and those of Gobush are very nearly identical to our results (see the immediately preceding equation).

This raises an important point. How does the lift force depend on the surface area of the ball? It makes sense also that the lift force should depend on other things, like the density and the viscosity of the air flowing past the ball. In order to properly discuss this, we need to digress briefly from our discussion of curve balls and talk about dimensional consistency.

◆ *Dimensionless Groups and the Lift Coefficient* ◆

From a scientific point of view, the immediately preceding equation is sloppy. The dimensions of quantities on either side of the equal sign in an equation must match. Since the force is in pounds, v is in feet per second, and ω in revolutions per minute, the constant 6.4×10^{-7} of the equation must have units of

$$\frac{\text{pounds} \times \text{seconds} \times \text{minutes}}{\text{feet} \times \text{revolution}}$$

Note that this constant does not have units related to properties of the ball or air density — properties, one would expect, affect the lift force. In general, this indicates that something is missing from the formulation. For example, as we indicated above, if we performed our experiments with a different-sized ball or in a different fluid, the "constant" should have a different value. We can get around this problem by the appropriate use of *dimensionless groups*. Let us begin our illustration of this idea with a somewhat far-fetched example of a familiar idea.

Suppose Galileo had performed the experiment in which he verified that the distance an object falls near the surface of the Earth is proportional to the square of the time elapsed. He would have measured

$$d = -16t^2$$

Had he the opportunity to perform his experiment on the Moon, he would have found that (approximately)

$$d = -2.6t^2$$

This is, of course, because the multiplier in front of t^2 is not really a constant. It has dimensions of length divided by time squared. Its value differs not only because the gravitational constant is different for the Earth and the Moon but, perhaps more importantly, its value is different when different units of length and time are used.

Notice that we can regroup the equation $d = 1/2\ at^2$ (with $a = -g$) as

$$\frac{d}{gt^2} = -\frac{1}{2}$$

The value of the constant on the right-hand side is $-1/2$, and it is truly constant, independent of whether the experiment is performed on Earth or on the Moon and independent of the units used. It is dimensionless, as is the *dimensionless group* d/gt^2. Scientists like to cluster their variables in dimensionless groups, especially when they are trying to make sense of experimental data. The constants that emerge are then *true constants*. Obviously, the variables that form the groups must have consistent units so that the groups themselves are dimensionless. For example, if d is in feet and g is in feet per second per second, then t must be measured in seconds.

It turns out that to fully describe that results of the lift force experiments three dimensionless groups are required. They are conventionally written as

$$\text{Group 1} = C_L = \frac{2F_L}{\rho A v^2}$$

$$\text{Group 2} = \text{SP} = \frac{R\omega}{v}$$

$$\text{Group 3} = \text{Re} = \frac{2vR}{v}$$

The quantity A in Group 1 is the cross-sectional area of the ball, R in Group 2 is the radius of the ball, ρ in Group 1 is the mass density of the air, and v in Group 3 is the kinematic viscosity of the fluid. The quantities A and R are obviously properties of the ball. Some clarifying comments are in order concerning ρ, the air density. It is common in many places to give the density of a gas or liquid in pounds per cubic foot. This is *weight density*. To get the *mass density* ρ, this must be divided by g. This is because mass is weight divided by g. A second comment is that $R\omega/v$ must be dimensionless. Since R has dimensions of length and v length per time, ω must have units of inverse time (1/time). We have previously used revolutions per minute for this quantity. To change this to 1/s, we note that one revolution is 2π radians (a radian is a dimensionless angular measure) and 1 minute is 60 seconds. Hence

$$1 \frac{\text{rev}}{\text{min}} \times \frac{2\pi \text{ rad/rev}}{60 \text{ s/min}} = \frac{\pi \text{ rad}}{30 \text{ s}}$$

To get radians per second from revolutions per minute, multiply by π and divide by 30. For example,

$$2000 \frac{\text{rev}}{\text{min}} = (2000) \times \frac{\pi}{30} = 209 \text{ rad/s}$$

The three dimensionless groups are related to one another in such a way that Group 1, which is called the *lift coefficient* and is denoted C_L, is a function of Group 2, which is called the *spin parameter* and is denoted SP. It has been shown experimentally that unless the ball is very smooth (much smoother than a baseball) C_L is not affected by Group 3. For higher speeds or for very smooth balls, like billiard balls, C_L would also be a function of Group 3, which is called the *Reynolds number*, after the British scientist Osborn Reynolds. It is written in the abbreviated form Re.

To show how well this works, we have plotted data points from several experiments performed by different people in different laboratories with different types of balls (Figure 25). Watts and Ferrer used real baseballs, Gobush used real golf balls, and Bearman and Harvey used a

FIGURE 25. *This figure shows lift data plotted in the way a scientist would plot it. The coordinates are the lift coefficient, C_L, and the spin parameter, SP, as explained in the text. Our data are plotted along with that of Gobush and that of Bearman and Harvey. Typical values of SP for baseballs range between 0.1 and 0.2. In this range C_L varies almost linearly with SP.*

dimpled ball somewhat like a golf ball but with 2¹/₂-times-larger diameter.

For a typical curve ball, ω is at most 2000 rev/min, or 209 rad/sec. Using a velocity of 85 mi/h (125 ft/s) and the radius of a baseball ($R = 0.119$ ft), we see that SP has a typical value of (0.119) (209)/ 125 = 0.2. We expect that it would seldom be greater. When SP is less than about 0.4, the relation between C_L and SP is almost a straight line of slope unity. Thus a good approximation is $C_L \approx$ SP, or

$$\frac{2F_L}{\rho A v^2} = \frac{R\omega}{v}$$

Replacing the cross-sectional area A with πR^2 and rearranging yields

$$F_L = {}^1/_2 \, \rho \pi R^3 \omega v$$

We can now see how the "constant" in the equation $F_L = 6.4 \times 10^{-7}$ ωv is related to the size of the ball and the density of the air. We can also see that the lift force varies directly with the product ωv.

As a final observation about dimensionless groups, we note how the data of Bearman and Harvey and the data of Gobush imply that we can use our results with confidence at larger ball speeds than we used in our experiments. Gobush tested balls at values of Re up to 2×10^5, and Bearman and Harvey as high as 2.38×10^5. Comparison of these values implies that our data are valid to speeds at least up to (2.38/0.8) = 2.98 times our maximum wind tunnel speeds, or up to 119 miles per hour.*

Now getting back to baseball, if we assume an 80-mph curve ball rotates at 209 rad/s, then using the equation $F_L = {}^1/_2 \, \rho \pi \, R^3 \, \omega v$ we can calculate

---

*Those readers who are intimately familiar with the Magnus effect—the phenomenon leading to the lift force on a spinning sphere—will realize that the physics can be more complicated than our explanation might lead one to believe. Under certain conditions the lift coefficient can depend strongly on the dimensionless group Re, which is called the *Reynolds number*. The lift can, under certain conditions, actually reverse in direction, for example. It turns out, however, that such strange phenomena, which are probably related to transition to turbulence of the boundary layer flow, only occur on smooth spheres. The seams on a baseball and the dimples on a golf ball make the balls much too rough for Magnus reversal to occur. While this is a fascinating topic deserving of scientific scrutiny, it is not relevant to our considerations here.

$$F_L = \frac{1}{2} (0.0023) \, \pi \, (0.0017) \, (209) \, (117) = 0.15 \text{ lbs} = 2.4 \text{ ounces}$$

which is in agreement with the equation derived using our original measurements.

◆ *Nonspinning or Slowly Spinning Baseballs: The Knuckle Ball* ◆

Systematic measurements of the forces on nonspinning baseballs have also been made. In 1968, Richard Gonzalez, a mechanical engineering student at Tulane University, measured the forces on a nonspinning baseball in a wind tunnel and reported the results in his bachelor's thesis. Two years later the measurements were carefully repeated and extended. The results were published in the *American Journal of Physics* by Watts and Sawyer.[10] Watts and Sawyer mounted a baseball on a device that could be used to measure the forces on the ball. The ball was then placed in a wind tunnel, initially in the position shown in Figure 26. With the ball oriented in this way, a drag force could be measured (in the direction of the wind velocity), but there was no force in the direction perpendicular to the wind direction (F_L in Figure 26). The ball

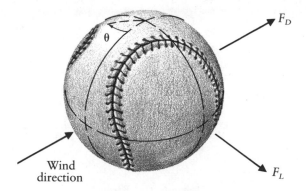

FIGURE 26. *To measure the forces on a spinless baseball, we mounted a ball in our wind tunnel in the position shown. The ball is shown oriented in a symmetric position relative to the position of the seams. The quantity θ is equal to zero. The ball was impaled on a thin vertical rod through its center. By turning it about the vertical axis, the seams could be oriented in various nonsymmetrical positions, and the forces measured by strain gages in the supports in much the same way that the spinning ball forces were measured.*

was then placed in different orientations by rotating it about the vertical axis (varying the angle θ in the figure). As expected, the nonsymmetrical locations of the seams caused a variation in the position of the wake, and the result was a sideward force F_L. Figure 27 shows how the magnitude of this force varied with the seams in different positions for a wind velocity of 68 feet per second (46 miles per hour). The force changes cyclically as the orientation is changed. A ball thrown with an orientation 30 degrees from the position shown in Figure 26 would be pushed to the left (from the pitcher's perspective) with a force of about 0.1 pound. A similar pitch with an orientation 60 degrees from that shown in Figure 26 would be pushed to the right with a force of about −0.1 pound. Thus, a pitch thrown without spin could curve to the right or to the left. In fact, if a pitcher was unlucky enough to throw a spinless pitch with the ball oriented perfectly symmetrically, it would not curve at all!

Obviously it is best if the pitch can be thrown with just a little rotation, because the direction of the force will change in midflight. This is why the knuckle ball's path is erratic. Figure 28 illustrates two cases, a knuckle ball thrown so that it rotates ¹/₄ turn on the way to home plate, and one that rotates ¹/₂ turn. The first begins curving toward the left and reverses itself. The second reverses itself *three times*. The more slowly rotating pitch has a maximum deflection that is much larger than that of the more rapidly rotating pitch. Remember that when a force is applied to a mass, it takes a little time to get the mass moving

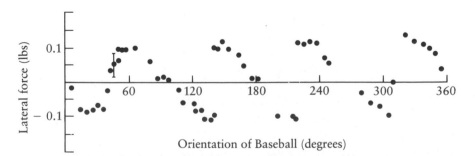

FIGURE 27. *The lateral (or sideward) force varies strongly with the orientation of the seams. A nonsymmetric location of the seams affects the flow in the boundary layer near the ball differently on different sides of the ball. This causes the wake to shift in one direction or another. When the wake shifts in one direction, a force is imparted on the ball in the other direction. The data shown here were made at a wind speed of 46 miles per hour.*

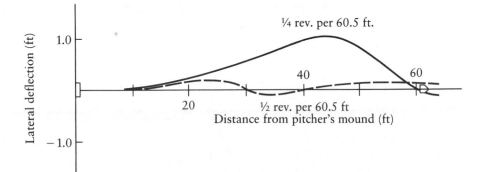

FIGURE 28. *If a pitch is thrown so that it spins very slowly, the lateral force on the ball will change in magnitude, and perhaps even in direction. The ball whose path is shown with a solid line was moving at 46 miles per hour and it rotated 90 degrees on the way to home plate. The lateral force, initially zero, increases to a magnitude of almost 0.1 pound. It then decreases in magnitude, reverses direction, and reaches about 0.1 pound in the other direction. If the ball rotates 180 degrees as shown with the dashed line, it reverses direction three times. Remember, though, that a force produces only an acceleration—a gradual change in velocity rather than an immediate change. If the force reverses too often, the ball doesn't have time to move very far. A good knuckle ball should rotate a little, but not too much.*

because it has to accelerate. The velocity does not change immediately. If the force changes direction too rapidly, the mass simply never gets anywhere. It turns out that the maximum displacement of a slowly rotating ball is

$$d_{\max} = \frac{g \times F_{L-\max}}{w\omega^2}$$

where F_{L-max} is the maximum force in pounds, w is the weight of the ball in pounds, and ω is the rotation rate in radians per second. This equation works only when the ball rotates at least $1/4$ revolution on its path to home plate. At rotation rates higher than about 2 or 3 revolutions on the way to home plate, a different phenomenon occurs, namely, that already described in our discussion of curve balls. When the ball rotates less than $1/4$ revolution, the force goes through less than one cycle (see Figure 27), and the above equation again cannot be used.

The lateral force shown in Figure 27 was obtained with a wind speed of 68 feet per second. However, Figure 29 gives an indication of how the maximum magnitude of the force, F_{L-max}, changes with the speed

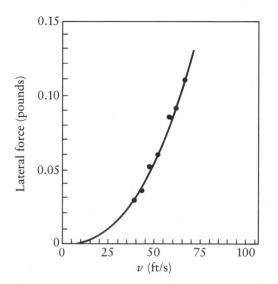

FIGURE 29. *The maximum lateral force on the spinless ball varies approximately with the square of the speed. If the maximum force on the ball as presented in Figure 27 at 46 miles per hour is 0.1 pound, the force on a typical 70 miles per hour knuckle ball is* $(70/46)^2(0.1) = 0.23$ *pound. Since it is moving faster, however, it has less time to move, and the* distance *it moves laterally will be the same as that shown in Figure 28. This is explained in the text.*

of the pitch (or the wind speed). This figure shows that the magnitude of the lateral force on the knuckle ball varies as the square of the speed. Its maximum absolute value is about 0.1 pound (i.e., varying from about 0.1 pound to the left to 0.1 pound to the right) when v is 68 feet per second. A major league pitcher might be expected to throw a knuckle ball a little faster, approximately 100 to 110 feet per second (70 to 75 miles per hour). At these speeds the magnitude of the maximum lateral force is 0.23 to 0.27 pound. An equation for the magnitude of the maximum lateral force is

$$F_{L-max} = 2.16 \times 10^{-5} \, v^2$$

where F_{L-max} is in pounds and v is in feet per second. In dimensionless terms, the lift coefficient C_L is constant with a value of 0.42. Hence, according to our dimensionless group arguments, since $C_L = 0.42$ the above equation can be written in the form

$$F_{L-max} = 0.21 \, \rho \, Av^2$$

◆ *Scuff Balls* ◆

Recently one of the authors (RGW) performed a set of experiments to measure the force on a "scuff ball." The cover of the ball was roughened by scratching it with a bottle top in one spot. This ball is shown in Figure 30. It was mounted in the wind tunnel so that the scuffed spot was on one side of the ball. It was not rotated. The lateral force on the ball in the direction of the scuffed spot is shown in Figure 31. Its value varied with the square of the wind speed as follows:

$$F_L = 1 \times 10^{-5} \, v^2$$

where F_L is in pounds and v is in feet per second. The lift coefficient is again constant, this time with a value of 0.194. Hence, for this particular scuff ball.

$$F_{L - max} = 0.097 \, \rho \, Av^2$$

FIGURE 30. *Scuff balls are prepared by scratching one part of the ball with a bottle cap, belt buckle, or whatever the pitcher can sneak to the mound. The ball is then thrown in such a way that the scuffed spot is at the axis of rotation of the ball. As the air flows around the ball the scuffed spot causes flow separation to be delayed, shifting the wake towards the side opposite the scuffed spot and inducing a force in the direction of the scuffed spot.*

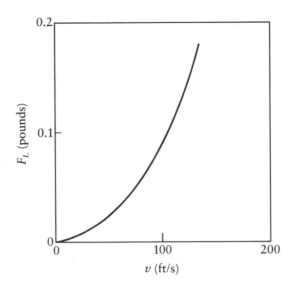

FIGURE 31. *The force on a scuff ball may be larger the more extreme the scuffing. Data for one particular ball are shown here. The force increases as the square of the velocity, reaching a value of about 0.17 pound at 90 miles per hour.*

◆ *How Far Do They Curve?* ◆

We have now discovered that the lateral forces on rapidly spinning and slowly spinning balls are similar in magnitude to those we used in some simple trajectory calculations in Chapter 2. Let us now explore some consequences of the way these forces vary with the speed of the pitch and the rotation rate of the ball. First consider the curve ball.

The most recent data (that of Watts and Ferrer and that of Bearman and Harvey) indicated that the lateral force on a curve ball is proportional to the speed of the pitch times the rotation rate. Thus, we can say that

$$F_L = C\,\omega v$$

where the constant C, according to the equation

$$\frac{2F_L}{\rho A v^2} = \frac{R\omega}{v}$$

is $\pi\rho R^3/2$. On the other hand, the equation

$$y = \frac{1}{2}\left[\frac{F_y g}{w}\right] t^2$$

tells us that such a force will move the ball in the lateral direction by a distance

$$d = \frac{F_L g t^2}{2w} = \frac{C \, \omega v g t^2}{2w}$$

Now, t is the time required for the ball to reach home plate, that is, the distance D to home plate divided by the speed v of the pitch. Thus,

$$t^2 = \frac{D^2}{v^2}$$

so that, from the equation

$$d = \frac{F_L g t^2}{2w} = \frac{C \, \omega v g t^2}{2w}$$

the total deflection of the curve ball is

$$d = \frac{\rho \pi R^3 \omega g D^2}{4wv}$$

Consistent units must be used in this equation of course; i.e., d in ft, ρ in lb-s/ft^4, R^3 in ft^3, ω in rad/s, g in ft/s^2, D^2 in ft^2, w in lb, and v in ft/s. This equation is illustrated in Figure 32. This equation shows that the faster the ball spins, that is, the higher ω, the further it will curve. Also, the *slower* the pitch, the further it curves. However, the slower pitch with more curve may be easier to hit than a fast pitch with less curve, because the batter has more time to track it and predict its trajectory.

Next, consider the knuckle ball. Let's suppose the ball is thrown so that it rotates N times on the way to home plate. The rotation rate is N revolutions per 60 feet multiplied by v feet per second multiplied by 60 seconds per minute, or

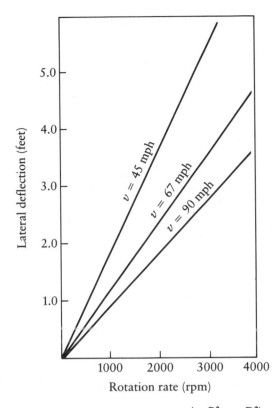

FIGURE 32. *An illustration of the equation* $d = \dfrac{(\rho\pi R^3 \ \omega g \ D^2)}{(4wv)}$. *The lateral force on a curve ball is directly proportional to the speed of the pitch and the square of the time to reach home plate. Since the time required to reach home plate is inversely proportional to the velocity, a slower pitch (at a given spin rate) curves further than a faster pitch. Of course the batter has more time to look at the ball when the pitch is slower.*

$$\omega \ \frac{\text{rad}}{\text{s}} = \frac{N \ \text{rev}}{60 \ \text{feet}} \times \frac{v \ \text{feet}}{\text{s}} \times \frac{2\pi \ \text{rad}}{\text{rev}} = \frac{Nv \ \pi}{30} \ \frac{\text{rad}}{\text{s}}$$

Thus, from the equation for maximum displacement,

$$d_{\text{max}} = 2920 \ \frac{F_{L-\text{max}}}{w(Nv)^2}$$

The value of F_{L-max} is given earlier. Combining that formula with the immediately preceding equation, we can see that

$$d_{max} = \frac{6.3 \times 10^{-2}}{wN^2}$$

If $N = 1/2$ and $w = 0.32$ pounds, then $d_{max} = 0.8$ feet. This equation is illustrated in Figure 33. The immediately preceding equation is not valid for $N < 0.25$. However, Hollenberg[11] has run computer simulations of knuckle balls with very low spin rates, for example, 3 rpm, and has found typical lateral displacements of 2 feet.

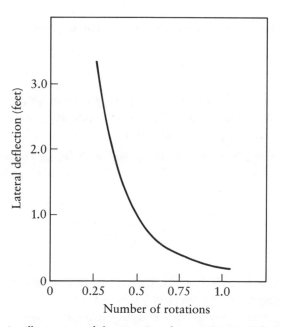

FIGURE 33. *An illustration of the equation $d_{max} = (6.3 \times 10^{-2})/(wN^2)$. Since the force on a knuckle ball depends on the velocity squared, the lateral deflection is independent of the speed of the pitch. It depends only on the rotation rate. Balls rotating by less than about 45 degrees, 1/8 of a revolution, on the way to home plate will generally curve in only one direction (that is, there will be no reversals). The larger the rotation rate of the ball, the more direction reversals will occur, but the smaller the maximum lateral distance the ball will move.*

The distance the knuckle ball moves is independent of velocity, a remarkable result. It shows that a fast knuckle ball will be deflected by the same distance as a slow knuckle ball. The deflection of a nearly spinless pitch is independent of the speed of the pitch. This may imply that a fast knuckle ball is better than a slow knuckle ball, because it will be deflected by the same distance but in a shorter period of time.

The same is true of the scuff ball. According to the equation

$$y = \frac{1}{2} \left[\frac{F_y g}{w}\right] t^2$$

$$d = \frac{F_L g t^2}{2w}$$

If we substitute F_L from the equation $F_L = 1 \times 10^{-5} v^2$ and the time t to reach home plate from equation $t^2 = D^2/v^2$, we find that for the particular scuffed ball used in our experiments,

$$d = 1.73 \text{ feet}$$

The distance the ball is deflected probably depends upon the size and roughness of the scuffed patch. However, once again this distance does not depend on the speed of the pitch.

We can summarize what we have learned as a set of graphs. Figure 32 is a graphical picture of the equation concerning the deflection of a curve ball:

$$d = \frac{\rho \pi R^3 \, \omega g \, D^2}{4wv}$$

Read in the rotation rate of the ball along the bottom, or horizontal, axis. Trace along a vertical line until you reach the straight line giving the speed of the pitch. Now go horizontally straight to the vertical axis on the left and read the deflection of the pitch.

Figure 33 is the same sort of thing for a knuckle ball, except this time the maximum deflection does not depend on the speed of the pitch. Read in the number of rotations on the way to the plate along the horizontal axis at the bottom. Trace a line up to the curve and then across to the left-hand vertical axis for the maximum deflection.

◆ *The Rising Fastball* ◆

In Chapter 3 we posed the question "Can a fastball rise?" as Walter Johnson's was reported to have done. Let us see what our measurements tell us. In order to rise, the ball must have enough backspin to induce a lift force larger than the weight of the ball, 5.125 ounces, or 0.32 pound. If we suppose that the ball is thrown at 147 feet per second (100 miles per hour), we can use the equation $F_L = 6.4 \times 10^{-7} \, \omega v$ to compute the required backspin. The result is

$$\omega = \frac{0.32 \text{ pound}}{(6.4 \times 10^{-7})(147 \text{ feet per second})} = 3400 \text{ rpm}$$

The maximum rotation rate of balls thrown by college baseball players reported by Selin was 2310 revolutions per minute. Can Nolan Ryan or Dwight Gooden make the ball spin 1100 revolutions per minute faster? Perhaps someday someone will have the opportunity to photograph a Ryan or Gooden fastball and count the revolutions. We think it is very unlikely.

We have spent the last three chapters discussing the pitcher's art and science. Yet pitchers are not the only players who manipulate the spin of the baseball to their advantage. According to Bill Shirley of the *Los Angeles Times*, Steve Garvey says the ball carries better if you undercut it a little. Clearly, what Garvey is proposing to do is put backspin on the ball to give it some lift. It is obvious that if the ball is undercut too much it will be popped up or fouled back. To understand how much is too much, and many other interesting things about the hitter's art and science, we need to turn our attention from the mound to the batter's box, as we do in the next chapter.

Notes

1. F. Verwiebe, "Does a Baseball Curve?" *American Journal Physics*, vol. 10, April 1942, pp. 119–120. A scientist's view.
2. R. G. Watts, and J. Walton, Gravity's Rainbows: The Kinematics of Baseballs and Bodies, Annual Meeting of the American Association for the

Advancement of Science, Detroit, May 1982. A speech to the American Association for the Advancement of Science on baseball, gymnastics, and diving.

3. C. Selin, "An Analysis of the Aerodynamics of Pitched Baseballs, *The Research Quarterly*, vol. 30, no. 2, 1959, pp. 232–240. High-speed pictures capture baseball spin.

4. L. J. Briggs, "Effect of Spin and Speed on the Lateral Deflection (Curve) of the Baseball; and the Magnus Effect for Smooth Spheres," *American Journal Physics*, vol. 27, 1959, pp. 589–596. Measurements of the forces on spinning balls.

5. J. H. Drury, "The Hell It Don't Curve," in *The Fireside Book of Baseball*, Charles E. Einstein (ed.), Simon and Schuster, New York, 1956. Baseball stories.

6. W. F. Allman, "Dance of the Curve," *Science81*, vol. 2, October 1981, pp. 90–91. Comments by scientists and players about curve balls.

7. P. Kirkpatrick, "Batting the Ball." *American Journal Physics*, vol. 31, 1963, pp. 606–613. A physicist looks at batting.

8. R. G. Watts and R. Ferrer, "The Lateral Force on a Spinning Sphere," *American Journal Physics*, 1987. Careful measurements of the forces on spinning balls.

9. P. W. Bearman and J. K. Harvey, "Golf Ball Aerodynamics," *Aeronaut Quarterly*, vol. 27, 1976, p. 112. Careful scientific measurements of the forces on spinning golf balls.

10. R. G. Watts and E. Sawyer, "Aerodynamics of a Knuckleball," *American Journal Physics*, vol. 43, 1975, pp. 960–963. A scientific account about why knuckleballs flutter and jump erratically.

11. J. W. Hollenberg, "Secrets of the Knuckleball," *The Bent of Tau Beta Pi*, vol. 77, no. 4, 1986, pp. 26–30. Measurements and computer calculations of knuckle ball motion.

Bat Meets Ball: Collisions

*I*t has been said many times that batting a baseball is the single most difficult act in all of sports. At the time of this writing only seven players in the combined major leagues are accomplishing the task of getting a base hit as often as once in every three attempts. Paul Kirkpatrick,[1] a physicist at Stanford University, pointed out that this is at least partly attributable to the fact that in the attempt to hit a baseball solidly with a bat there are so many things that can go wrong. Let us suppose that for a given pitch there is an ideal way for the bat to meet the ball in a collision. This means that there is an ideal location of the bat at the instant that the collision occurs. The location of the bat is determined by three variables: its height above the ground, its position along a line between home plate and the pitcher's mound, and its position in the direction across home plate. There is also an ideal angular position of the bat (three more variables), an ideal speed (three more, one component in each direction), and an ideal angular speed (still three more). Obviously, if the batter adjusts all these things perfectly, but swings too early or too late, it would do his cause no good. Thus, he can also fail in his task through the mismanagement of time. Taken together with the fact that any of the above 13 variables can be missed on either the high side or the low side, this means that there are 26 ways to fail.

Not all the variables are equally important, of course. A baseball bat is a more or less cylindrical object, and its correct position when it strikes a baseball is approximately horizontal and perpendicular to the path of the approaching ball. A small error in the rotational position of the bat about a vertical axis may cause an otherwise perfectly hit home run to go into the left or right field bleachers instead of the center field bleachers, while a larger error would transform a home run into a long but harmless foul ball. On the other hand, an error in the rotational position about the axis (length) of the bat is of no importance at all. The most critical variable is the vertical position of the bat. Conventional wisdom is that a very tiny error here (a few millimeters) can spell the difference between success and failure. However, we will scrutinize this few millimeters assumption in the last section of this chapter and again in Chapter 6.

An interesting aspect of the game of baseball is the fact that the batter, the offensive player, is not essentially in control of the ball. This is a situation quite different from that in any other sport played with a ball. In baseball, the defensive team controls the ball perhaps 95 percent of the time. The hitter's job is to hit the ball in such a way that the defensive team loses control long enough for him or one of his team-mates to circle the bases. A team scores not so much by controlling the ball as by forcing his opponents to lose control. The ultimate method of doing this is to hit the ball in such a way that it goes out of the playing field (from fair territory) as a home run. In a sense, the batter has momentarily gained full control of the ball and the defensive team has completely lost control. Even as the ball is thrown toward the batter's box, the pitcher has a certain amount of control over the path of the ball. The batter's task of causing the defensive team to lose control is made more difficult because the pitcher can manipulate the path of the ball in a way presumably known only to himself and the catcher. In addition to imposing a variety of forces on the ball by both legal and illegal means, most pitchers expose batters to some added psychological stress by occasionally reminding them how much a baseball thrown at 85 to 95 miles per hour hurts when it hits them. Most batters already know this, of course, so the reminder can be indirect. Ryne Duren, a flamethrowing relief pitcher for the New York Yankees during the 1960's, sometimes warmed up by throwing several pitches over the catcher's head. He would then remove his thick glasses and, while wiping them with his handkerchief, squint at the batter taking his place in the batter's box. Thus, another variable, fear (ball players use the term *respect*), enters the batter's formula for failure.

Hitting a baseball can be thought of as consisting of four interrelated parts: seeing the ball as it approaches and deciding whether and where to swing the bat, actually swinging the bat, the collision between the ball and the bat, and the path, or trajectory, of the ball after it leaves the bat. In this chapter, we will discuss only the third of these, the collision between the bat (a modified right circular cylinder) and the ball (a sphere). In Chapter 6 we will discuss the trajectory of the ball after it leaves the bat. In Chapter 7 we will study the head and eye movements of a batter trying to follow a pitch.

◆ *Momentum, Impulse, and Collisions* ◆

In order to explain the collision process, we must introduce another idea from physics: the concept of momentum. The momentum principle stems directly from Newton's second law:

$$F = Ma$$

Suppose a constant force F is applied to an object of mass m so that its speed increases from v_0 to v over a time interval t. Since the average acceleration is the change in speed divided by the change in time,

$$F = m\,\frac{v - v_0}{t}$$

or, after rearranging the terms,

$$Ft = mv - mv_0$$

The quantity mv is the *momentum* of the object; mv_0 is its initial momentum, and mv is its momentum after a force F has been applied to it for a time t. The quantity Ft is called the *impulse*. The impulse on an object during a collision is equal to the change of momentum resulting from the collision. If there is no force, the momentum remains unchanged.

Consider now what happens when two objects (a bat and a ball) collide head on. To simplify matters, we will assume the ball and bat velocity vectors are colinear, as shown in Figure 34. Assume the ball has mass m_1 and speed v_{1b}, and the bat has mass m_2 and speed v_{2b} before the collision. Since the collision is head on, v_{1b} and v_{2b} are in opposite directions. This is indicated in the figure by placing a minus sign in front of the ball's velocity, v_{1b}. In a typical collision of bat and ball the force is very large and the time period over which the forces act is very small. These forces greatly deform one or both objects. The deformations cannot, however, be seen by the naked eye because they happen so fast. Figure 35 is a picture of a baseball-bat collision taken with a high-speed camera. The baseball, being considerably softer than the bat, is deformed to a surprising degree during the collision. It is obviously subjected to a very large force. The force can be as large as 1500 pounds for a period as short as 0.002 second. After this time interval, the force

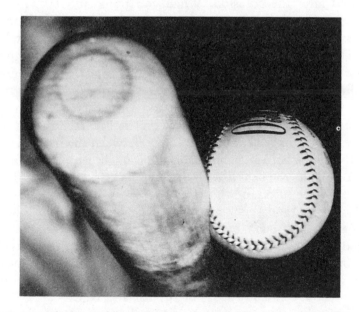

FIGURE 34. *A collision between a ball (on the right and moving toward the left in the top diagram) and a bat (on the left and moving toward the right). The subscript 1 is for the ball, 2 is for the bat. The subscript b is for before the bat-ball collision (the top diagram), and a is for after the collision (the bottom diagram). [Adapted from A. T. Bahill and W. J. Karnavas,* Biological Cybernetics, 62:89–97, 1989.]

FIGURE 35. *A high-speed flash photograph of a bat striking a baseball. Notice the deformation of the ball, indicating the enormous magnitude of the impulsive force at this instant. [Courtesy Harold E. Edgerton, Massachusetts Institute of Technology, Cambridge, Mass.]*

between the ball and bat returns to 0 and the ball springs back to its nearly spherical shape. According to another law of motion, Newton's third law, if the force imposed by the mass m_2 on the mass m_1 during the collision is F_1, then the force imposed by m_1 on m_2 is $-F_1$. Using F_1 in the equation for the principle of momentum the third equation on page 86 gives

$$F_1 t = m_1 v_{1a} - m_1 v_{1b}$$

Since the ball is moving to the left, v_{1b} is a negative number. Similarly, applying the momentum principle to the mass m_2 gives

$$-F_1 t = m_2 v_{2a} - m_2 v_{2b}$$

Adding the right- and left-hand sides of these equations and rearranging, we can see that

$$m_1 v_{1b} + m_2 v_{2b} = m_1 v_{1a} + m_2 v_{2a}$$

The *total* momentum of the two objects taken together is the same before and after the collision. When you think about it, this is not surprising. Each object exerts a force on the other, but these forces cancel, and there is no net force on the two objects when taken together. The equation represents the law of the conservation of momentum: the total momentum must remain unchanged, when there is no externally applied force.

In the collision between a baseball and a bat there *is* another force, the force that the batter's hands exert on the bat. If, however, it were anywhere near as large as the force acting between the bat and the ball, it would sting the batter's hands badly. This might happen, for example, when the ball hits the bat close to the batter's fists. Usually (if the ball is hit properly) the effect of the force from the batter's hands on the collision is small, and the immediately preceding equation is accurate. There is another problem, however. If the collision between the ball and the bat does not occur at the bat's center of mass, the collision will induce rotational motion in the bat. We will consider such collisions in the last section of this chapter. For now we will consider only the velocities of the centers of mass of the bat and ball.

The immediately preceding equation tells us a lot about head-on collisions, but it cannot tell us all we want to know. Usually in collision problems we know the masses m_1 and m_2 and the speeds v_{1b} and v_{2b} of the two objects before the collision. We wish to determine the speeds

v_{1a} and v_{2a} of the objects after the collision. There are two unknowns. We cannot find them both from only one equation. To determine either of the speeds after the collision we need another equation.

We need an equation that describes the physical characteristics of the two bodies that are colliding. Clearly, it's going to make a great deal of difference whether, object m_1 is a baseball or a lump of clay, and whether m_2 is a wooden bat or a foam-rubber pillow. In other words, the "bounciness" of both objects is involved. A baseball will bounce higher when dropped on a concrete floor than will a softball or a lump of clay. None of these will bounce high when dropped on a thickly carpeted floor.

The property that scientists use to describe the "bounciness" associated with the collision between two objects is the coefficient of restitution e. Its value is

$$e = \frac{\text{relative speed after collision}}{\text{relative speed before collision}}$$

In our case,

$$e = -\frac{v_{1a} - v_{2a}}{v_{1b} - v_{2b}}$$

To get some feeling for what this equation tells us, let us construct a simple example. Suppose we drop an object (of mass m_1) on a concrete floor (of mass m_2). In this special case both v_{2b} and v_{2a} are obviously zero (the concrete floor does not move either before or after the collision) and

$$e = -\frac{v_{1a}}{v_{1b}}$$

Suppose the object strikes the floor at -10 feet per second (negative because it is going down). If the ball-concrete combination were perfectly "bouncy," $e = 1$, the floor would just reverse the ball's direction, and v_{1a} would be $+10$ feet per second. Conversely, a ball of clay would not bounce at all. In that case, $e = 0$. The baseball-bat collision lies somewhere between these two extremes. The manufacture of baseballs is carefully controlled to ensure that the coefficient of restitution is 0.55. From the definition of the coefficient of restitution and from the equations of Chapter 2, it can be seen that if you drop a professional league baseball onto a concrete floor, it will rebound e^2 of the original distance; for example, if you drop it from 6 feet, it will rebound about 22 inches. Brancazio[2] has shown that the coefficient of restitution depends somewhat on the velocities of the objects before the collision, but these effects are so small that we will use a constant value of e throughout this book. Assuming e to be constant also makes the mathematics much simpler.

◆ *The Standard Major League Baseball* ◆

A baseball is currently required to weigh between 5 and 5.25 ounces and to have a diameter between 2.86 and 2.94 inches. Before 1973 major league baseballs had been for many years assembled in the Spalding factory in Chicopee, Massachusetts. Then the work was done for a few years in Haiti, and since 1976 in Taiwan. The balls are constructed in layers. At the center is a composition cork ball encased in two thin layers of rubber, one black and one red. On this is tightly wound 121 yards of blue-gray wool yarn, 45 yards of white wool yarn, another 53 yards of blue-gray wool yarn, 150 yards of fine cotton yarn, and a coat of rubber cement. It is enclosed in a cowhide cover — hand-stitched with 216 red cotton stitches.

The weight and diameter of a baseball have been standardized since 1872, when machines for the manufacture of balls came into use. However, this did not solve the problem of standardizing the coefficient of restitution of the balls. A debate over this elusive physical property has been going on at least since the 1860's, when Henry Chadwick charged that the baseballs in use at the time were "overelastic." During those early years, the color, texture, and "liveliness" of the balls varied widely according to team preference. There were many manufacturers of baseballs. Almost every city sporting a baseball team had at least one.

In 1875, the Ryan "dead-ball" was adopted as the official baseball. However, in 1876 Albert G. Spalding and his brother J. Walter Spalding of Spalding Bros., Inc., began manufacturing a ball with uniform specifications, and in 1878 the Spalding League Ball became the official baseball of the National League. The balls were *given* to the league. In fact, Spalding Bros., Inc. paid the league $1 a dozen for the privilege. The advertising paid off handsomely. When the company began operating, it boasted $800 in capital. By 1892, it had absorbed several of the largest sporting goods companies and had a capital stock worth $4 million.

◆ *Why Are There More Home Runs Now?* ◆

In the 1950's the tidal wave of home runs renewed speculation about the coefficient of restitution. Was the ball getting livelier? It is indeed true that home run–hitting increased consistently after the early 1900's. Figure 36 is a graph showing how the number of home runs per game per team has changed from year to year. A value of 0.2 means that teams hit an average of two home runs every ten games, or one homer in every five games played that year. This number increased dramatically between about 1920 and 1960, reaching a value around 0.8, which translates into about 3 or 4 percent of the balls hit in fair territory being home runs. Note the steep rise in the home run rate between 1919 and 1922, the decline during World War II, and the recovery after the war. Recently there has been another sharp rise.

The reason or reasons for the long-term increase in the number of home runs is difficult to pin down. Unfortunately (although Spalding Bros., Inc. claimed the manufacturing methods and materials were standard), actual quality control through regular measurements of the coef-

FIGURE 36. *The average number of home runs has increased throughout the years.*

ficient of restitution had not been practiced before the mid-1950's. In an article in *Collier's* magazine, Tom Meany[3] reported that Spalding Bros., Inc. claimed that there had been no changes in the specifications in manufacturing their baseballs for at least three decades. Conversely, there is a National Bureau of Standards report stating that official major league balls in 1943 were found to have coefficients of restitution of 0.41. It has been speculated that during World War II, the quality of the material used in the manufacture of baseballs was inferior to that used in other years. This coefficient of restitution of 0.41 is much lower than the value of 0.55 that is required of the present-day ball. The fact that the home run explosion was already well on its way by the 1940's casts some doubt on the "livelier ball" theory.

The year 1987 was a banner year for home run hitting, and speculations about the increased coefficient of restitution continued to abound. Baseball manufacturers continued to deny allegations of "rabbit" balls. *USA Today* reported on July 3, 1987, that tests of 1987 and 1977 baseballs performed by Haller Testing Laboratories showed only the slightest changes. The coefficient of restitution has, according to their results, *declined* by 0.4 percent during that 10-year period.

A more reasonable explanation of what is behind the trend toward more and more home runs is the "livelier ball player" theory. It was Babe Ruth who really started the trend toward more home runs in 1919. When it was pointed out to Ruth in 1930 that he made more money than President Hoover, Ruth reportedly responded, "I had a better year." Home run hitters generally began having much better years (financially) than those who merely hit singles for higher averages. As Meany said, "The money's in the big end of the bat." Hitters are concentrating more on hitting home runs. As is the case in other sports, diet and other factors have also led to healthier, stronger players.

◆ The Best Bat Weight: From the Principles of Physics ◆

The bat might have played at least as important a role as the ball in the home run explosion. According to statistics compiled by Hillerich and Bradsby, manufacturers of the Louisville Slugger bat, the average weight of bats used by top players decreased from about 40 ounces in the

1920's to about 32 ounces in the 1950's.[3] This was a period during which home run production increased dramatically. However, not all batters follow the same trend. According to Dan Gutman in a 1988 *Discover* article,[4] to make the bat heavier "Ted Kluszewski of the Cincinnati Reds used to sink tenpenny nails into his bat barrel. St. Louis Browns first baseman[6] George Sisler banged in Victrola needles." To make the bat lighter, many players, including Houston's Billy Hatcher and Detroit's Norm Cash, have drilled a big hole in the end of the bat and filled it with cork. In an attempt to change the coefficient of restitution some players have stuffed the bat with Super Balls. Gutman[4] says, "Back in 1974 Graig Nettles of the Yankees took a vicious swing in the fifth inning of a game against Detroit, splitting his bat as it made contact. Out bounced six Super Balls." Brancazio[2] cites an article in *Newsday* magazine saying that "a hitter sometimes hollows a bat and stuffs it with a spongy substance like cork or rubber balls to make the bat expand explosively . . . upon impact with a ball." This is nonsense, as pointed out by Brancazio. In fact, as long as the structural integrity of the bat is not destroyed by drilling too large a hole, the coefficient of restitution of the bat-ball collision is unchanged. Note that the outer surface of the bat shown in Figure 35 is undeformed during the collision with the ball. A change in the coefficient of restitution of the ball-bat combination is almost certainly not responsible for the most recent increase in home run hitting. In the remainder of this chapter and in Chapter 6 we will explore some other possibilities. Let us now see what the theory of collisions can say about this important question.

Now that we have some understanding of the coefficient of restitution, or the "bounciness" that occurs when bat meets ball, we have a way of relating the speeds of two objects before and after the collision to the physical properties of the colliding objects. This allows us to use the equation for conservation of momentum

$$m_1 \, v_{1b} + m_2 \, v_{2b} = m_1 \, v_{1a} + m_2 \, v_{2a}$$

with the equation for the coefficient of restitution

$$e = -\frac{v_{1a} - v_{2a}}{v_{1b} - v_{2b}}$$

to obtain expressions for both the bat and ball speed immediately after the collision. We find that

$$v_{1a} = \frac{(m_1 - em_2)\, v_{1b} + (m_2 + em_2)\, v_{2b}}{m_1 + m_2}$$

and

$$v_{2a} = \frac{(m_1 - em_1)\, v_{1b} + (m_2 + em_1)\, v_{2b}}{m_1 + m_2}$$

Much can be learned from these two equations, so let's dwell on them for awhile.

First, since v_{1b} is a negative number and v_{2b} is a positive number (the objects are moving in opposite directions), v_{1a}, the speed of the ball after the collision, always increases with e. Also, as long as $m_1 - em_2$ is negative (the weight of the bat is larger than $1/e$ times the weight of the ball), v_{1a} increases when $-v_{1b}$ increases. This means that fastballs can be hit harder than slow pitches, all other things being equal.

Finally, the equation for v_{1a} tells us that, all other things being constant, the speed of the ball as it leaves the bat increases as the weight of the bat increases. Suppose, for example, that the bat is much lighter than the ball. Omitting the term m_2 from the immediately preceding equations, that is, assuming m_2 is close to zero, shows that in that case

$$v_{1a} = v_{1b}$$

which means the ball zooms past with undiminished speed. We also find that

$$v_{2a} = (1 - e)\, v_{1b} + ev_{2b}$$

(the bat flies backwards). Suppose, on the other hand, that the bat weighs very much more than the ball. In such a case, terms involving m_1 in the equations for v_{1a} and v_{2a} can be dropped. The results are then

$$v_{1a} = -ev_{1b} + (1 + e)v_{2b}$$

and

$$v_{2a} = v_{2b}$$

The collision with the ball does not affect the speed of the huge bat. *For a given bat speed*, this is the largest velocity that can be imparted to the ball. According to this reasoning, bats should be as heavy as the rules will allow.

There is, of course, a problem with this kind of analysis. A little thought tells us that if the bat is too heavy, the batter cannot control it well enough to make good contact with the ball. Even if he could make contact with the ball, the bat speed before contact would be smaller than that which could be attained with a lighter bat. What the analysis above does not account for is that the larger m_2, the smaller the bat speed before the collision, v_{2b}. What we have here is a case of conflicting effects.

This is as good a time as any to introduce a much-overlooked fact about the practical use of scientific theories. Scientific ideas can be used to explain what is happening in the world around us, and, in many cases, to predict better ways of doing things. But we must be quite specific in the way we ask questions. Almost all really interesting scientific problems involve conflicting factors. In the case of hitting a baseball with a bat, we found that, strictly from the point of view of momentum considerations, the speed of a baseball leaving the bat with a given bat speed is maximized by making the bat mass (or weight) as large as possible. A very large bat would, however, be hopelessly unwieldy. From the standpoint of bat control and accuracy the bat should be extraordinarily light. The equation

$$v_{1a} = v_{1b}$$

and the equation

$$v_{2a} = (1 - e)v_{1b} + ev_{2b}$$

as well as our intuition tell us that such a bat would simply be knocked from a batter's hands. Surely there is an optimum bat weight between these two extremes. But optimum in what sense?

Momentum effects associated with the collision itself tell us that for a given speed, we need a massive bat. We also know, however, that the smaller the bat, the higher the bat speed that can be obtained. The speed with which a particular batter can swing his weapon depends on how much energy he can put into his swing. To resolve our conflict, and to learn more about the optimum bat and the optimum swing, we need to stop looking at only the bat and the ball. We must now consider the human being swinging the bat.

◆ The Best Bat Weight: From the Principles of Physics and Physiology* ◆

The speed of a baseball after its collision with a bat depends on many factors, not the least of which is the weight of the bat. One professional baseball team (St. Louis Cardinals) says the weight of the bat is determined by "the player's personal preference"; another (New York Yankees) says, "Each individual player determines the style of bat he prefers." These players have very little real scientific data to help them support their preferences. In this section we present data to help an individual player to decide if his or her preference is the most effective bat weight. Knowing the ideal bat weight can eliminate time-consuming and possibly misleading experimentation by ball players.

To find the best bat weight we must first re-examine the conservation of momentum equations for bat-ball collisions. For the science of baseball the distinction between mass and weight is not critical, and so we will substitute weight for mass in the equation for the conservation of momentum to produce

$$w_1 v_{1b} + w_2 v_{2b} = w_1 v_{1a} + w_2 v_{2a}$$

Keep in mind that we are assuming the weight of the batters arms has no effect on the collision (this may be an important assumption). We want to solve for the ball's speed after its collision with the bat — called the *batted-ball speed* — but first we should eliminate the bat's speed after the collision, because it is not easily measured. We can use the equation for the coefficient of restitution to solve for v_{2a}, substitute the result into the equation for the conservation of momentum, and solve for the ball's speed after its collision with the bat. The result is

---

*This section was based on Bahill and Karnavas.[5]

$$v_{1a} = \frac{(w_1 - ew_2)v_{1b} + (w_2 + ew_2)v_{2b}}{w_1 + w_2}$$

This means that the ball's speed after the collision will depend on the weight of the ball and bat, the coefficient of restitution, and the precollision speeds of the ball and bat.

Kirkpatrick[1] assumed that the optimal bat weight would be the one that "requires the least energy input to impart a given velocity to the ball." This definition in conjunction with the immediately preceding equation yields

$$\left[\frac{w_2}{w_1}\right]_{\text{optimal}} = \frac{v_{1a} - v_{1b}}{v_{1a} + ev_{1b}}$$

If we now make the reasonable assumptions that

$w_1 = 5.125$ oz, the weight of the ball

$e = 0.55$, the coefficient of restitution of a baseball

$v_{1b} = -80$ mph, a typical pitch speed

$v_{1a} = 110$ mph, the ball speed needed for a home run

we can solve the immediately preceding equation to find that the *optimal bat weight* is 15 ounces!

Brancazio[2] has written an excellent theoretical analysis of bat-ball collisions. He considered not only the bat's translation but also its angular rotation about two axes. He found that the ball's speed after the collision with the bat depends on

1.   the energy imparted by the body and arms;

2.   the energy imparted by the wrists;

3.   the speed of the pitch;

4.   the point of collision of the ball with respect to

   a.   the center of percussion,

   b.   the center of mass,

    c.   the end of the bat,

    d.   the maximum energy transfer point, and

5.   the weight of the bat

However, by assuming that a professional baseball player exhibited normal values for each of these dependencies, he also concluded that the *optimal bat weight* is about 15 ounces.

These conclusions cannot help professional baseball players, who must use solid wood bats, because a 15-ounce solid wood bat would only be about 15 inches long! Such a bat would be far smaller than any bat that is now used in professional baseball. A typical major league bat weighs about 32 ounces. Babe Ruth normally used a 44-ounce bat, and sometimes used bats weighing more than 50 ounces. On the other hand, a fungo bat, a bat used for hitting fly balls in practice sessions, weighs about 23 to 24 ounces. One might take this to mean it is closer to the optimum weight. However, a fungo bat is used to hit balls that have initial speeds v_{1b} of practically zero, so a re-examination of the conservation of momentum equation indicates that for that case, the bat should weigh the same as the ball, about $5^{1}/_{4}$ ounces.

These conclusions may help explain why people choke up on the bat; choking up makes the bat effectively shorter, moves the center of mass closer to the hands, thereby reducing the moment of inertia, and in essence makes the bat act like a lighter bat. Several reasons have been advanced for buying a long bat and choking up on it. First, a longer bat must be made from wood that has straighter grain. Therefore bat manufacturers use the best wood for the longer bats, and bats made from the best wood do not break as easily. Secondly, using a longer bat allows the batter to change the effective weight of the bat during his time at bat. Al Rosen recalled that Ted Williams and Mickey Mantle did not choke up with no strikes. If the pitcher got one strike on them, they choked up a half inch. If the pitcher got two strikes, they choked up an inch. This conclusion could also help explain the great popularity of aluminum bats. The manufacturers can make them lighter while maintaining the same length and width.

It might also explain why so many professional players are "corking" their bats.[4,6] "Players," says Stephen Hall in an issue of *Science83* magazine, "have been known to drill a half-inch diameter hole in the fat end of the bat—anywhere from eight to fourteen inches deep—and . . . fill it with cork." Norm Cash freely admits to having used a corked bat in 1961, when he won the American League batting title by batting .361. Presumably, he also used a corked bat in 1962 when he only hit .243. The advantage of corking the bat is that it makes the bat lighter. For some batters this is advantageous.

Both Kirkpatrick's and Brancazio's physics studies were limited by their explicit assumptions. Kirkpatrick assumed that the optimal bat was the one that required the smallest bat kinetic energy. Brancazio's calculations of the optimal bat weight were based on the assumption that the "batter generates a fixed quantity of energy in a swing," independent of the bat weight. We will now extend these studies by allowing the amount of energy imparted to the bat by the batter to depend on bat weight.

Physiologists have long known that muscle speed decreases with increasing load.[7-10] This is why bicycles have gears. The rider can keep muscle speed in its optimal range while bicycle speed varies greatly. Therefore, to discover how muscle properties of individual ball players affect their best bat weights, we measured the bat speeds of many batters swinging bats of various weights. We plotted the data of bat speed versus bat weight, and used this to help calculate the best bat weight for each batter.

◆ *The Bat Chooser™ Instrument* ◆

Our instrument for measuring bat speed, the Bat Chooser,* has two vertical light beams, each with associated light detectors (similar to the electric eyes on elevator doors). The subjects were positioned so that when they swung the bats the center of mass of each bat passed through the light beams. A computer recorded the time between interruptions of the light beams. Knowing the distance between the light beams and the time required for the bat to travel that distance, the computer calculated the speed of the bat's center of mass for each swing. Our computer sampled every 16 microseconds. In all cases our velocities are accurate to better than 1%.

Each player was positioned so that bat speed was measured at the point where the subject's front foot hit the ground. This is the place where most players reach maximum bat speed and therefore where they hit the ball with maximum force.

---

*Bat Chooser is a trademark of Bahill Intelligent Computer Systems. A patent is pending.

We told the batters to swing each bat as fast as possible while still maintaining control. We told the professionals to "pretend you are trying to hit a Nolan Ryan fastball."

In our experiments each adult subject swung six bats through the light beams. The bats varied from superlight to superheavy, yet they had similar lengths and weight distributions. In our developmental experiments we tried about three dozen bats. We used aluminum bats, wood bats, plastic bats, infield fungo bats, outfield fungo bats, bats with holes in them, bats with lead in them, major league bats, college bats, softball bats, Little League bats, brand new bats, and bats over 40 years old. In one set of experiments we used the six bats shown in Figure 37 and described in Table 2. These bats were about 35 inches long, with the center of mass about 23 inches from the end of the handle of each bat.

For Little League players we changed to a different set of bats. They had to be lighter and fewer in number. For our final experiments we used the set described in Table 3. However, even with this set we saw signs of fatigue in half our subjects.

In a 20 minute interval of time, each subject swung each bat through the instrument five times. The order of presentation was randomized.

TABLE 2 Characteristics of the Six Adult's Bats

Name	Weight (oz)	Length (in)	Distance From the End of the Handle to Center of Mass (in)	Composition
F	49.0	35.0	22.5	Aluminum bat filled with water
E	42.8	34.5	24.7	Wood bat, drilled and filled with lead
D	33.0	35.5	23.6	Regular wood bat
C	30.6	34.5	23.3	Regular wood bat
B	25.1	36.0	23.6	Wood fungo bat
A	17.9	35.7	21.7	A wooden bat handle mounted on a threaded steel lamp pipe with a 6-oz weight attached to the end

[From A. T. Bahill and W. J. Karnavas, *Biological Cybernetics*, 62:89–97, 1989.]

FIGURE 37. *The bats used in our final experiments; the lightest is on the left, the heaviest on the right. These bats are described in Table 2. (Photo: Richard Harding).*

Name	Weight (oz)	Length (in)	Distance to Center of Mass (in)	Composition
TABLE 3 Characteristics of the Four Boy's Bats				
A	40.2	29.9	17.8	Wood bat with iron collar
B	5.2	31.3	17.6	Plastic bat
C	25.1	28.0	17.3	Wood bat
D	21.1	28.8	17.0	Aluminum bat

[From A. T. Bahill and W. J. Karnavas, *Biological Cybernetics*, 62:89–97, 1989.]

The selected bat was announced by a DECtalk® speech synthesizer; for example, "Please swing bat Hank Aaron, that is, bat A." We recorded the bat weight and the linear velocity of the center of mass for each swing.

◆ The Force-Velocity Relationship of Physiology ◆

When bat speeds measured with this instrument were plotted as a function of bat weight, we obtained the typical muscle force–velocity relationship shown in Figure 38. The ball-speed curve and the term *Ideal bat weight* shown in this figure will be discussed in a later section. This

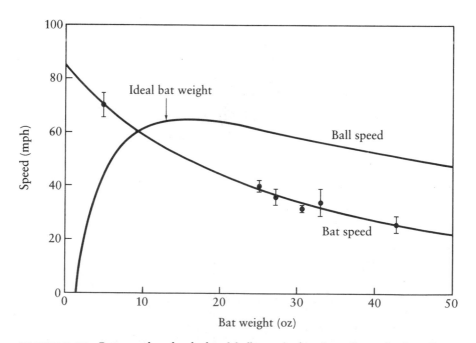

FIGURE 38. *Bat speed and calculated ball speed after the collision both as functions of bat weight for a 40-mph pitch to Alex, a ten-year-old Little League player. The dots represent the average of the five swings of each bat; the vertical bars on each dot represent the standard deviations. These data were collected with a different set of bats than that described in Table 3. [From A. T. Bahill and W. J. Karnavas, Biological Cybernetics, 62:89–92, 1989.]*

force-velocity relationship shows that the kinetic energy ($\frac{1}{2} mv^2$) put into a swing was zero when the bat weight was zero, and also when the bat was so heavy that the speed was reduced to zero. The bat weight that allowed the batter to put the most energy into the swing, the *maximum-kinetic-energy bat weight*, occurred somewhere in between. This led to the suggestion that the batter might choose a bat that would allow maximum kinetic energy to be put into the swing. Figure 39 shows the kinetic energy as a function of bat weight for a member of the San Francisco Giants. This batter could impart the maximum energy to a bat weighing 46.5 oz.

This maximum-kinetic-energy bat weight does not, however, tell us the bat weight that will make the ball leave the bat with the highest speed. To calculate this weight we must couple the muscle force–velocity relationship to the equations for conservation of momentum. We can then solve the resulting equations to find the bat weight that

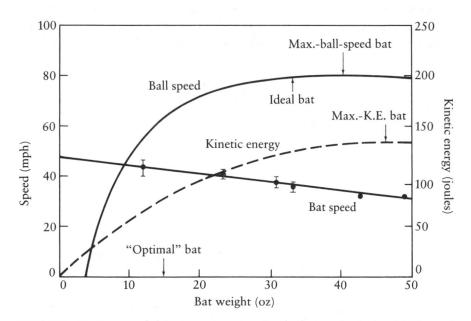

FIGURE 39. *Bat speed, kinetic energy given to the bat, and calculated ball speed after the collision, all as functions of bat weight for an 90-mph pitch for a member of the San Francisco Giants baseball team. Data for other professional baseball players were similar. These data were collected with a different set of bats from that described in Table 2. [From A. T. Bahill and W. J. Karnavas,* Biological Cybernetics, 62:89–97, 1989.]

would allow a batter to produce the greatest batted-ball speed. This would, of course, make a potential home run go the farthest, and give a ground ball the maximum likelihood of getting through the infield. We call this weight the *maximum-batted-ball-speed bat weight*.

◆ Coupling Physics to Physiology ◆

Next we coupled the equations of physics to the equations of physiology. Over the last half century physiologists have used three equations to describe the force-velocity relationship of muscles: that for the straight line ($y = Ax + B$), that for the hyperbola ($[x + A][y + B] = C$), and that for the exponential ($y = Ae^{-Bx} + C$).[11] Each of these equations has been best for some experimenters, under some conditions, with certain muscles, but usually the one for the hyperbola fits the data best. In our experiments we fit all three and chose the equation that gave the best fit to the data of each subject's 30 swings. For the data of Figure 39, the best fit was: bat speed (in mph) $= -0.34$ bat weight (in oz) $+ 48$, or

$$v_{2b} = -0.34w_2 + 48$$

Next we substituted this relationship into the equation

$$v_{1a} = \frac{(w_1 - ew_2)v_{1b} + (w_2 + ew_2)v_{2b}}{w_1 + w_2}$$

yielding

$$v_{1a} = \frac{(w_1 - ew_2)v_{1b} + (w_2 + ew_2)(Aw_2 + B)}{w_1 + w_2}$$

We then took the derivative with respect to the bat weight, set this equal to zero, and solved for the maximum-batted-ball-speed bat weight. The result is

$$w_{2mbbs} = \frac{-w_1A - \sqrt{w_1{}^2A^2 - Aw_1(B - v_{1b})}}{A}$$

For the data of Figure 39 this was 40.5 oz.

The physics of bat-ball collision predicts an optimal bat weight of 15 oz. For the professional baseball player of Figure 39, the physiology of the muscle force–velocity relationship reveals a maximum-kinetic-energy bat weight of 46.5 oz. When we coupled the equation $v_{2b} = -0.34w_2 + 48$, fit to the force-velocity data of Figure 39 to the equation derived from the coefficient of restitution and the principle of conservation of momentum for bat-ball collisions, we were able to plot the ball speed after the collision as a function of bat weight, also shown in Figure 39. This curve shows that the maximum-batted-ball-speed bat weight for this subject was 40.5 oz, which is heavier than that used by most batters. However, this ball speed curve is almost flat between 34 and 49 oz. There is only a 1.3 percent difference in the batted-ball speed between a 40.5-oz bat, and the 32-oz bat normally used by this player. Evidently the greater control permitted by the 32-oz bat outweighs the 1.3 percent increase in speed that could be achieved with the 40.5 oz bat.

◆ *Ideal Bat Weight™* ◆

The maximum-batted-ball-speed bat weight is probably not the best bat weight for any player. A lighter bat will give a player better control and more accuracy. Obviously a trade-off must be made between maximum batted-ball speed and controllability. Because the batted-ball speed curve of Figure 39 is so flat around the point of the maximum-batted-ball-speed bat weight, we believe there is little advantage in using a bat as heavy as the maximum-batted-ball-speed bat weight. Therefore, we have defined the *Ideal Bat Weight** to be the weight at which the ball speed curve drops 1 percent below the speed of the maximum-batted-ball-speed bat weight. Using this criterion, the ideal bat weight for this subject is 33 oz. We believe this gives a reasonable trade-off between distance and accuracy. Of course, this is subjective and each player might want to weigh the two factors differently. It does, however, give a quantitative basis for comparison. The player of Figure 39 was typical of the San Francisco Giants players whom we studied, as shown in Table 4,

---

*Ideal Bat Weight is a trademark of Bahill Intelligent Computer Systems.

TABLE 4 Summary of Data for the 28 San Francisco Giants							
Maximum Batted-ball Speed (mph)		*Ideal Bat Weight (oz)*		*Actual Bat Weight (oz)*		*Maximum Kinetic Energy (joules)*	
Average	Range	Average	Range	Average	Range	Average	Range
99	80–122	31.7	26.25–37.00	32.3	31–34	270	133–408

except that his swings were slower but more consistent than most. He is a control hitter.

For contrast, in Figure 40 we show the data of a San Francisco slugger who was less consistent. However, his slugging average was over .600. His data are best fit with bat speed (in mph) = −0.39 bat weight (in ounces) + 63. Substituting this into the equation for v_{1a} and performing our other calculations yield an ideal bat weight of 32 ounces. It is surprising that although the two players and their data as shown in Figures 39 and 40 are so dissimilar, their ideal bat weights are nearly the

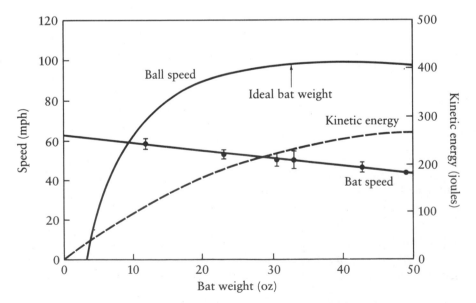

FIGURE 40. *Bat speed, kinetic energy, and calculated ball speed after the collision, for a different member of the San Francisco Giants baseball team.*

TABLE 5 Measured Ideal Bat Weight				
Team	Mean Ideal Bat Weight (oz)	Standard Deviation	Pitch Speed	Number of Subjects
San Francisco Giants	31.7	3.8	90	28
University Baseball	28.3	2.8	80	11
University Softball	27.8	3.7	60	12
Little League	20.1	3.4	40	11
Slow Pitch Softball	19.4	1.0	20	4

[From A. T. Bahill and W. J. Karnavas, *Biological Cybernetics*, 62:89–97, 1989.]

same. These data contrast dramatically with data from the 10-year-old boy of Figure 38. His data are best fit with this hyperbola:

$$(w_{bat} + 28.0) \times (\text{bat speed} + 12.8) = 2728$$

Substituting this into the equation for v_{1a} and performing our other calculations yields an ideal bat weight of 15 ounces.

The ideal bat weight varies from person to person. Table 5 shows the means and standard deviations of ideal bat weights for batters in various organized leagues. These calculations were made with the pitch speed each player was most likely to encounter, for example, 40 mph for Little League and 20 mph for university professors playing slow pitch soft-ball.* Ideal bat weight is specific for each individual, but it does not appear to be correlated with height, weight, age, circumference of the upper arm, or any combination of these factors, nor is it correlated with any other obvious physical factors.

To further emphasize the specificity of the ideal bat weight calculations, we must display individual statistics rather than averages and standard deviations. In Figure 41 we compare the ideal bat weight with the weight of the actual bat used by the players before our experiments. This figure shows that most of the players on the San Francisco Giants baseball team are using bats in their correct range. The dashed lines in this figure (derived from data and calculations not shown in this chap-

---

*The coefficient of restitution of a softball is smaller than that of a baseball, but this did not affect our calculations, because the ideal bat weight is independent of the value of the coefficient of restitution.

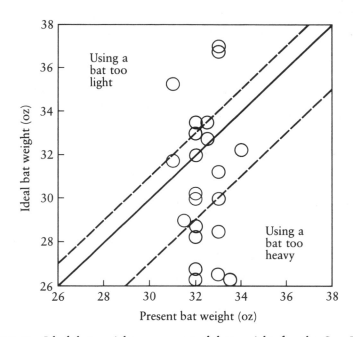

FIGURE 41. *Ideal bat weight versus actual bat weight for the San Francisco Giants. Most of them are using bats in their recommended range. [From A. T. Bahill and W. J. Karnavas,* Biological Cybernetics, *62:89–97, 1989.]*

ter) delineate the range of bat weights that we recommended to their management. We recommended that batters above the upper dashed line switch to heavier bats and that batters below the lower dashed line switch to lighter bats.

Not only is the ideal bat weight specific for each player, but it also depends on whether the player is swinging right- or left-handed. We measured two switch-hitters (one professional and one university ball player). One player's ideal bats weights were 1 ounce different and the other's were 5 ounces different. Switch-hitters were so different when hitting right- and left-handed that we treated them as different players.

Extrapolating from the equation

$$w_{2mbbs} = \frac{-w_1 A - \sqrt{w_1^2 A^2 - A w_1 (B - v_{1b})}}{A}$$

shows that the ideal bat weight also depends on pitch speed. Figure 42 shows this dependence of ideal bat weight on pitch speed for the ball

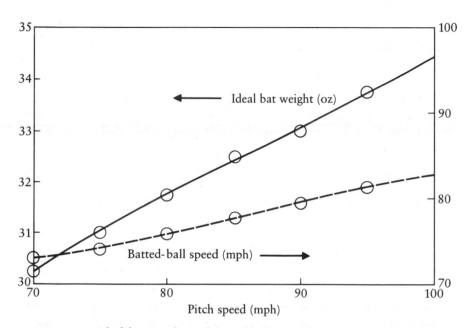

FIGURE 42. *Ideal bat weight and batted-ball speed both as a function of pitch speed for the professional baseball player of Figure 39. [Adapted from A. T. Bahill and W. J. Karnavas,* Biological Cybernetics, 62:89–97, 1989.]

player of Figure 39. This figure also shows the resulting batted-ball speed after a collision with a bat of the ideal weight. Such curves were typical of all our subjects.

This figure shows that the ideal bat weight increases with increasing pitch speed. This means that even if they could swing 33-oz bats, Little Leaguers should use lighter bats, because the pitch speeds are lower. However, when this figure is used to identify the ideal bat weight for a particular individual, the results may seem counterintuitive. When the opposing pitcher is a real fireballer, the coach often says, "Choke up [i.e., get a lighter bat] so you can get around on it." In such situations the coach is changing the subjective weighting of bat control versus distance. He is asking the player to drop his criterion to 2 or 3 percent below maximum-batted-ball-speed bat weight so he can get better bat control. Since the batted-ball speed depends on both the pitch speed and the bat weight, the batter can afford to choke up when facing a fast pitcher, knowing that the ball will go just as far as it would if he were not to choke up when facing a slower pitcher.

One more result that came from our studies is that proficient batters have consistent swings. They are machine-like. They train this machine-like precision. Compare the height of the data crosses (the standard deviation) of the swings of the Little League player of Figure 38, who had been playing ball for five years, with the height of the crosses for the swings of the professional player who had been playing ball for 24 years (Figure 39). Consistency is important and the professional player shows this consistency.

◆ *Generalizations and Limitations* ◆

It is not surprising that in a game that is more than 100 years old, played by players who are being paid hundreds of thousands of dollars per year, that professional athletes, without the benefit of scientists and engineers, have found that their best bat weights are between 30 and 34 ounces. However, it is interesting to note that, given the relative newness of the aluminum bat and the fact that the players using aluminum bats are amateurs, Little League and slow-pitch softball players cannot yet get bats that are light enough for them. The lightest Little League–approved bat that we have seen is 21 ounces. The lightest legal softball bat that we have seen is 27 ounces. (However, these numbers are decreasing at the amazingly high rate of about an ounce per year.)

For the Little Leaguer of Figure 38 the batted-ball speed varies greatly with bat weight. This means that it is very important for him to have the correct weight bat. However, for most professional baseball players, once the bat is in the correct range, the batted-ball speed varies little with bat weight, as shown in Figure 39. That player could use any bat in the range 33 to 40 ounces and there would be less than a 1 percent change in batted-ball speed. This fact is not in the literature and it could not be determined accurately by experimentation by ballplayers on the ball field. For example, imagine an experiment where a pitcher alternately throws 20 white balls and 20 yellow balls to a batter who alternately hits with a 32- and a 34-oz bat. Imagine then going into the outfield and looking at the distribution of distances of the balls. You would not see the yellow balls or the white balls consistently farther out. Variability in the pitch and the location of the contact point between the bat and the ball would obscure any differences. However, with our instrument we can accurately measure bat speed and calculate the resulting batted-ball speed. Our calculations show that this curve is flat. This knowledge should help professional batters eliminate futile experimentation with bat weights, while attempting to get higher batted-ball speeds. As long as the player uses a bat in the flat part of his curve, there will be less than a 1 percent variation in batted-ball speed caused by varying bat weights. What does a 1 percent decrease in batted-ball speed mean? A ball that would normally travel 333 feet would only travel 330 feet. This is not terribly important.

In our studies we measured bat speed as a function of bat weight. Next, we coupled these measurements to the equations of physics and physiology to determine the ideal bat weight for each individual batter. We can say nothing about the "feel" of a bat; this is a psychological variable that we cannot measure. We cannot say anything about the grain or strength of the bat. In this study we say little about choking up on the bat. We treat a 33-oz bat choked up 1 inch as a 32-oz bat. We are not concerned with the availability of bats. Our recommendations are independent of what equipment is actually available. We have tried to make sure that our solutions to tomorrow's problems are not stated in terms of the hardware that was available yesterday. We have no means of assessing the accuracy of the swing. Throughout our analysis we assume that it is easier to control a lighter bat than a heavier one.

In this study we measured the linear velocity of the center of mass of the bats. It is obvious that in addition to this translation the bat also rotates about two different axes. However, our results derived from only linear velocity agree in most details with those Brancazio derived using angular velocity. The exception is that for a rotating bat, the place where the ball hits the bat becomes important, as will be shown. If the ball hits the bat at its center of mass, the results of the linear approximation are the same as those derived treating translation and rotation separately. However, if the ball hits the bat 6 inches closer to its end, then the ideal bat weight would increase 2 ounces for the Little Leaguer of Figure 38, and 3 ounces for the major leaguer of Figure 39. All in all, we think our approximation of linear velocity is reasonable. We will return to this issue in the next section of this chapter.

We have also neglected the effect of air resistance on pitch speed. We calculated the ideal bat weights of the major league players based on a pitch speed of 90 mph. If the ball was going 90 mph when it hit the bat, it would indeed be a fast pitch, because the ball loses about 10 percent of its speed on its way to the plate. If we decreased our 90-mph figure by 10 percent, the ideal bat weights would decrease by approximately one ounce.

Our data have low variability for physiological data. For the data of

Figure 39 the standard deviations are about ±5 percent. However, the repeatability of our experiments is not as good. On any given day the data are repeatable, but tests run 1, 2, or 12 months apart differ by as much as 20 percent in bat speed for any given bat. However, in spite of these large differences in bat speed, the calculated ideal bat weight varies by only an ounce or two. We are still looking for the sources causing the lack of repeatability. We think the most likely causes are warm-up status, adrenaline, positioning of the subject, and fatigue.

Our experiments were done indoors. Some of the ball players thought things would be different out on the field swinging against a real pitcher. To study this effect we took the equipment out to the ball field. Immediately after an intrasquad game, we measured the bat speeds of four players while they hit the ball. For each player these data fell within the range of his data collected in the laboratory six months earlier and one week later.

◆ Two Types of Force-Velocity Curves ◆

We found two classes of batters: those whose force-velocity relationships were fit best with straight lines (like Figure 39), and those that were fit best with hyperbolic curves (like Figure 38). The data of the Little Leaguer shown in Figure 38 are fit best with this hyperbola: (w_{bat} + 28.0) × (speed + 12.8) = 2728. The data of his brother, also a Little Leaguer, collected on the same day are fit best with a straight line. Most Little Leaguers were fit best with hyperbolas, half of our college players were fit best with hyperbolas, and one-fourth of our major leaguers were fit best with hyperbolas.

The data for two more San Francisco Giants are shown in Figure 43. The top figure is for a quick player (a short stop/third baseman): the hyperbolic fit (solid line) is 35 percent better (in a mean squared error sense) than the straight line fit (dotted line). The bottom figure is for a nonquick player (an outfielder); his data are fit best with a straight line. Both of these players have maximum batted-ball speeds above 110 mph (in Chapter 6 we show that 110 mph is needed for a home run). And indeed both of these players have hit more than 20 home runs in a season.

The two professional players of Figure 43 both normally used 33-ounce bats. As shown in this figure, they swung our 31- and 33-ounce

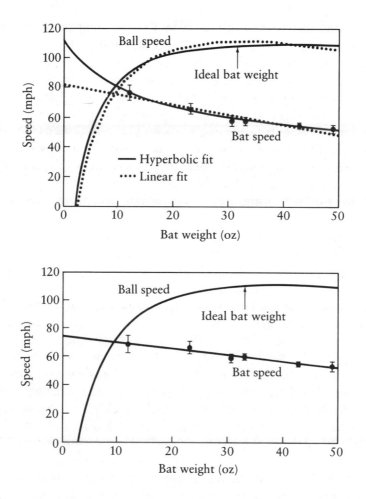

FIGURE 43. *Bat speed and batted-ball speed as functions of bat weight for an 90-mph pitch for two different members of the San Francisco baseball team. The player of the top graph was "quick," the player of the bottom graph was not. These data were collected with a different set of bats than that described in Table 2. [Adapted from A. T. Bahill and K. J. Karnavas,* Biological Cybernetics, 62:89–97, 1989.]

bats at the same speed. Within the limits of statistical variability, we can say that for bats in the range that they normally use, the two players swing with the same speed. However, our recommendations for these two players were quite different. We recommended that the player of the bottom figure keep his 33-ounce bat, but that the player of the top figure change to a 31-ounce bat. Why did this happen? In our experiments we gave them very heavy and very light bats, unlike any bats they have ever encountered. From the data collected with their swinging these bats we made mathematical models of each human, for example, the solid lines of Figure 43. From these models we made predictions about each individual's ideal bat weight. Modeling is a common scientific technique. Scientists and engineers build models and use the models to make predictions about the physical world. That is what we have done here. We have made models of the individual players and have used these models to predict their ideal bat weights. Such predictions could not be made using just experimental data from bats that they normally use.

We tried to correlate the type of curve that gave the best fit (i.e. straight line or hyperbola) with height, weight, body density, arm circumference, present bat weight, batting average, slugging average, running speed, etc., but had no success. However, we noted that the subjects who were fit best with hyperbolas were described by their coaches as being "quick." Quickness is not the same as running speed, but it is related. Quickness is easy to identify but hard to define. Shortstops, centerfielders, and lead-off batters are usually quick. Coaches easily identified their quick players, but when asked to explain why they called these players quick, they waffled. Their uneasy verbalizations include phrases like "they react quickly," "they move fast," "they steal many bases," "they get into position to field the ball quickly," "they swing the bat fast," and "they beat out bunts." But all these phrases describe resulting behavior, not physiological characteristics. So we decided to measure eye-hand reaction time and try to correlate it with the bat swing data. Eye-hand reaction time was measured by:

1. Holding a meter stick in front of a subject. Instructing him to place his opened index finger and thumb at the 50-cm mark and to watch the fingers of the experimenter, who holds the end of the meter stick.

2. Having the subject close his fingers as quickly as possible when the experimenter releases the meter stick and it begins to fall.

3. Noting the place where the subject catches the meter stick. The place indicates eye-hand reaction time ($d = 1/2\ at^2$).

4. Giving each subject two warm-up trials, and then collecting data for ten trials.

5. Selecting the median value of these ten trials as our measure of quickness.

The median eye-hand reaction time for the quick boy of Figure 38 was 143 ms; for his nonquick brother it was 256 ms. We collected eye-hand reaction times for 21 of the San Francisco Giants and compared it with the percentage superiority of the hyperbolic fit over the straight line fit. We found that the physiologic parameter that best differentiates between players whose data can be fit best with a straight line and those who require a hyperbola is the eye-hand reaction time.

For our nonquick subjects the weight of the bat seemed to have little effect on how they swung it. They swung all bats with about the same speed, and their data were fit best with a straight line, as shown in the bottom graph of Figure 43. For our quick subjects the weight of the bat was a limiting factor; speed depended on weight. The curves had steep slopes and needed hyperbolas to fit the data, as shown in the top graph of Figure 43. We hypothesize that the quick people change their control strategies when given different bats; whereas nonquick people do not change their strategies — they swing all bats the same way.

◆ Résumé ◆

The physics of bat-ball collisions without consideration of physiology (specifically the equations for conservation of momentum and the coefficient of restitution) predicted an *optimal bat weight* of 15 ounces. The physiology of the muscle force–velocity relationship showed that the professional baseball player of Figure 39 could put the most energy into a swing with a 46-oz bat; that is, the *maximum-kinetic-energy bat weight* was 46 ounces. Coupling physics to physiology showed his *maximum-batted-ball-speed bat weight* to be 40 ounces. Finally, trade-offs between maximum ball speed and controllability showed that his *ideal bat weight* was 33 ounces. These experiments explain why most adult batters use bats in the 28- to 34-oz range, they explain the variability in human choice of bat weight, and they suggest that there is an ideal bat weight for each person.

◆ *Rotational Motion of the Bat* ◆

This section is highly technical and may be skipped without losing continuity. The equation for acceleration,

$$F = m \, \frac{v - v_0}{t}$$

the equation for conservation of momentum,

$$m_1 v_{1b} + m_2 v_{2b} = m_1 v_{1a} + m_2 v_{2a}$$

and the intervening equations on pages 86 and 88 are true as long as the velocities in those equations are the velocities of the centers of mass of the two bodies. The momenta in this case are called *linear* or *translational* momenta. The sum of the translational momenta of two colliding objects is always conserved during a collision. However, the swing of a baseball bat exhibits two types of motion: translational and rotational. This is illustrated in Figure 44. To move the bat from position *A* to

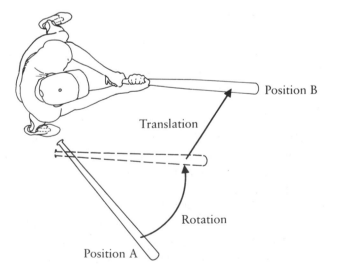

FIGURE 44. *The batter imparts two types of kinetic energy to the bat: rotational and translational.*

position *B*, one can first *rotate* the bat about the center of mass and then *translate* the center of mass. Each type of motion has associated with it a type of kinetic energy. The kinetic energy of translation is

$$KT = \frac{m_2 v_{2c}^2}{2}$$

where m_2 is the mass of the bat and v_{2c} is the speed of the center of mass of the bat. The kinetic energy of rotation is

$$KR = \frac{I_c \omega_c}{2}$$

where ω_c is the rotation rate about the center of mass and I_c is the moment of inertia. The moment of inertia is related to the mass of the bat and its shape. In swinging a baseball bat *KR* is usually much smaller than *KT*.

As we have seen, another theorem from physics, the work–kinetic energy theorem, tells us that when work is done on a body, kinetic energy is produced in an amount equal to the work done:

$$\text{Work} = KT + KR$$

Clearly, there is some maximum amount of kinetic energy that a given player can put into the swing of a bat. Furthermore, one can imagine that the more effort put into maximizing the kinetic energy of the bat, the less bat control the hitter has.

In order to understand the importance of this rotational motion, we must pause for a moment and consider how rotational and translational motion are related and how forces create rotational motion.

First consider the general case shown in Figure 45 in which a rigid body of arbitrary shape is supported at a point *A*, which we take to be its center of rotation. Suppose a force *F* is applied at a point *B* at a distance *H* from *A* and in a direction perpendicular to a line joining *A* and *B*. The product *HF* is called the *torque T*. We are interested in how the torque produces rotational motion about the point *A*.

First note that if the bar rotates about the point *A* the speeds of different points on the body will be different. In fact, a little thought reveals that a point, P_1, that is twice as far from *A* as another point, P_2,

FIGURE 45. *When a force is applied at point* B *and the bat is pivoted at point* A, *the bat will acquire angular momentum* ω.

will move twice as far along a circular arc as will point P_2 in a given time. Therefore, P_1 must move twice as fast as P_2. In general,

$$\frac{\text{Speed of point } P_1}{\text{Speed of point } P_2} = \frac{\text{distance from } A \text{ to } P_1}{\text{distance from } A \text{ to } P_2}$$

The *angular velocity* ω is defined as

$$\omega = \frac{v}{D}$$

where v is the translational speed at any point on the body and D is the distance from A to that point. By comparing the two immediately preceding equations, we can see that the angular velocity is the same at all points on the rigid body. The angular velocity must be given in dimensions of radians per second, where one rotation per second is equal to 2π radians per second.

When a torque is applied to a body, the equation for acceleration

$$F = \frac{v - v_0}{t}$$

cannot be applied directly because each point on the body is moving at a different speed. However, since the rotational velocity is the same at all points on the body, we can take a different approach. We view the body as being made up of a large number of small masses, Δm, each located at a distance r from the center of mass. The momentum of each piece is then $\Delta m \times r \times \omega$. And the *angular momentum* of each piece is defined as $r \times \Delta m \times r \times \omega$, or $\Delta m \times r^2 \times \omega$, and the sum of the angular momenta of all the pieces is called the angular momentum of the body:

$$AM = \Sigma \ (r^2 \ \Delta m \times \omega)$$

The symbol Σ means "sum of." Since ω is the same for each piece,

$$AM = \omega \times \Sigma \ r^2 \ \Delta m$$

Just as a force operating over time creates momentum, a torque T creates angular momentum. This is described mathematically by an equation similar to the equation for acceleration:

$$Tt = (\omega - \omega_0) \ \Sigma r^2 \Delta m$$

If the initial angular momentum is $\omega_0 \Sigma r^2 \Delta m$, the angular momentum after time t, when the torque T is applied, is $\omega \Sigma r^2 \Delta m$.

The quantity $\Sigma r^2 \Delta m$ is clearly a function of both the mass of the object and the *distribution* of the mass. It will require more torque to speed up (in rotational motion) an object having most of its weight far from its center of mass than an object with most of its weight close to its mass center because $\Sigma r^2 \Delta m$ will be larger in the former than in the latter. The quantity $\Sigma r^2 \Delta m$ is given a special name; it is called the *moment of inertia* about the center of mass or I_0.

When a real baseball player swings a real bat, the motion of the bat consists of a combination of two rotational motions, one centered in the batter's body and the other in the batter's wrists. We are now in a position to reconsider the baseball-bat collision accounting for these rotational motions. The following discussion follows the analyses of Brancazio[2,12] and Brody.[13] Referring to Figure 46, we designate the distance from the center of rotation of the batter's body to his wrists as R, and we consider this distance to be constant, although it surely varies somewhat during the batter's swing. Similarly, we designate the distance from the wrists to the center of mass of the bat as H and the distance from the center of mass of the bat to the point where the ball hits the bat as B. The angular velocity of the batter's body and arms is ω_{body}, so the linear velocity of his hands at a distance R from his body is

$$v_{hands} = R \ \omega_{body}$$

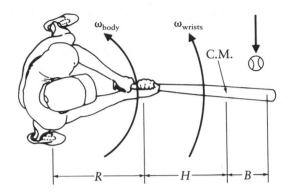

FIGURE 46. *A batter swinging a bat will produce rotations of the bat with both his body and his wrists. CM designates the center of mass of the bat.*

The velocity of the bat's center of mass due to the rotation of his body and arms is $(R + H)\omega_{body}$, while the velocity of the center of mass due to wrist rotation is $H\omega_{wrists}$. The sum of these is the velocity of the center of mass of the bat. Using the symbol v_{2b} for the velocity of the center of mass of the bat before collision, as we did earlier in this chapter,

$$v_{2b} = (R + H)\,\omega_{body} + H\omega_{wrists}$$

Following the same reasoning, the velocity of the point B due to ω_{body} is $(R + H + B)\omega_{wrists}$. Hence the velocity of point B, the point of contact between the bat and ball, is

$$v_B = (R + H + B)\omega_{body} + (H + B)\omega_{wrists}$$

This means (combining the two immediately preceding equations) that

$$v_B = B(\omega_{body} + \omega_{wrists}) + v_{2b}$$

and this tells us that the motion of the point of contact B can be envisioned as the sum of two motions, one of which is the translational motion of the center of mass and the other a rotation of the bat about the center of mass with angular velocity $\omega_2 = \omega_{body} + \omega_{wrists}$, where as before the subscript 2 stands for the bat.

Notice that if the point of impact were at the center of mass of the bat, v_B and v_{2b} would be the same (because B would be zero) regardless of the rotational velocity of the bat. If, on the other hand, the ball and bat do not collide at the center of mass of the bat, a change in the rotational velocity of the bat will occur. This change in angular velocity is the result of torque, just as the change in linear (translational) velocity in the equation

$$F = \frac{v - v_0}{t}$$

resulted from a force. Suppose the force exerted on the bat during the collision is $-F_1$ and the force on the ball is F_1. The torque on the bat about its center of mass is $-BF_1$ and, equating this torque multiplied by the time of its application to the change in angular momentum of the bat, we find that

$$-BF_1t = I_0(\omega_{2a} - \omega_{2b})$$

where ω_{2a} is the angular velocity of the bat (about its center of mass) after the collision and ω_{2b} is its angular velocity before the collision, $\omega_{body} + \omega_{wrists}$. For the ball,

$$BF_1t = Bm_1 (v_{1a} - v_{1b})$$

which is the same as equation

$$F_1t = m_1 v_{1a} - m_1 v_{1b}$$

since we are here assuming the collision occurs at the center of mass of the ball. Obviously most collisions will not occur at the center of mass of the ball, and, therefore, the ball will obtain rotational as well as translational kinetic energy. However, in typical bat-ball collisions the rotational kinetic energy is at most 3 percent of the translational kinetic energy. Therefore, neglecting the rotational kinetic energy of the ball is reasonable. Adding the equations

$$-BF_1t = I_0 (\omega_{2a} - \omega_{2b})$$

and

$$BF_1 t = Bm_1 (v_{1a} - v_{1b})$$

and noting that the sum is zero because angular momentum is conserved during a collision, we find that

$$I_0 (\omega_{2a} - \omega_{2b}) + Bm_1 (v_{1a} - v_{1b}) = 0$$

The immediately preceding equation and the equation

$$m_1 v_{1b} + m_2 v_{2b} = m_1 v_{1a} + m_2 v_{2a}$$

are both true during a bat-ball collision, as is the equation

$$e = \frac{\text{relative speed after collision}}{\text{relative speed before collision}}$$

However, the equation

$$e = - \frac{v_{1a} - v_{2a}}{v_{1b} - v_{2b}}$$

is not the correct expression for the coefficient of restitution because the relative velocities there represent those of the centers of mass of the ball and bat and not the velocities at the point B, where the collision takes place. The correct expression is

$$e = - \frac{v_{1a} - v_{2a} - B\omega_{2a}}{v_{1b} - v_{2b} - B\omega_{2b}}$$

The equations

$$m_1 v_{1b} + m_2 v_{2b} = m_1 v_{1a} + m_2 v_{2a}$$
$$I_0 (\omega_{2a} - \omega_{2b}) + BM_1 (v_{1a} - v_{1b}) = 0$$
$$e = \frac{v_{1a} - v_{2a} - B\omega_{2a}}{v_{1b} - v_{2b} - B\omega_{2b}}$$

can be solved simultaneously and after a good deal of algebra we find that

$$v_{1a} = \frac{-v_{1b}\left[e - \dfrac{m_1}{m_2} - \dfrac{m_1 B^2}{I_0}\right] + (1 + e)(v_{2b} + B\omega_{2b})}{1 + \dfrac{m_1}{m_2} + \dfrac{m_1 B^2}{I_0}}$$

Comparing the above equation to the following translation only equation

$$v_{1a} = \frac{(m_1 - em_2)\,v_{1b} + (m_2 + em_2)\,v_{2b}}{m_1 + m_2}$$

shows that the two are identical when $B = 0$, as they should be. This equation has been previously derived by Brancazio[2,12] (using different symbols). He also gives a lengthy and interesting discussion of what the equation can tell us about the effects on hitting of the various values in the equation. Of particular interest is the variation of v_{1a}, the batted-ball speed, with B, the distance from the center of mass of the bat to the collision point, and with $\sqrt{I_0/m_2}$, a measure of the mass distribution, or shape, of the bat. Brancazio has calculated the values of $\sqrt{I_0/m_2}$, which is called the *radius of gyration* about the center of mass for various bats. Some of his data are presented in Table 6. The W1 refers to a typical wood bat; A1, to an aluminum bat with a wall thickness of 0.1255 inch that has the same shape and weight as W1; an A2 to an aluminum bat of the same shape as A1 but with a wall thickness of 0.1 inch. From this table we see that a 31-oz, 34-in wooden bat has a smaller radius of gyration than either a 31-oz or a 25-oz aluminum bat of equal length. Brancazio says, "In general . . . it is to the batter's advantage to select

TABLE 6 Properties of Some Bats			
	W1	A1	A2
Length (in)	34	34	34
Weight w (oz)	31	31	25
Distance from the end of the handle to the center of mass (in)	21.9	19.6	19.5
Moment of inertia about the center of mass, I_0 (lb-ft-s^2)	0.0354	0.0432	0.0353
Radius of gyration k_0 (in)	9.2	10.2	10.2

a bat with a large value of k_0." Next, Brancazio calculated the value of B that resulted in the maximum value of v_{1_a}. This is the collision point for which the bat imparts maximum energy to the ball. He calls it the *maximum energy transfer* or *MET point*. It is important to note that the MET point is *not*, as is commonly believed, the center of percussion of the bat.

Let us first investigate how v_{1_a} varies with the collision point for two bats of equal weight, one a wooden bat and the other an aluminum bat. In each case, we assume the total bat kinetic energy before the collision is 300 foot-pounds per second (or 408 joules) which, as is shown in Table 5, is the largest value recorded for the San Francisco Giant players. The results are shown in Figure 47. There are several interesting features in these two curves. First, the speed of the ball leaving the bat is about 120 mph, which is greater than home run speed. Second, the MET point is closer to the handle for the aluminum bat than for the wood bat. Finally, and perhaps the most important point of all, the curve is significantly broader for the aluminum bat. As pointed out by Brancazio, this has some important implications regarding hitting with wood and aluminum bats.

The MET point for an aluminum bat is closer to the handle than the MET point for a similar wood bat. More importantly, the effective hitting surface is slightly shorter toward the barrel end, and much longer near the handle for an aluminum bat. This means that aluminum bats are much more effective for hitting inside pitches. Those who have hit with both aluminum and wood bats report that this is true. The principal reasons for this are that k_0, the radius of gyration about the center of mass, is larger for aluminum bats and the center of mass itself is closer to the handle. Brancazio has performed a similar analysis for corked bats and reported that corking the bat does not help. It would appear, however, that there might be some bat design applicable to wooden bats that would increase the value of k_0, while still maintaining the general requirement that the bat be cylindrical and made of solid wood. The best *shape* of a wooden bat has almost certainly not yet been determined.

◆ *Oblique Collisions: Putting Spin on the Ball* ◆

Until now we have dealt only with a head-on collision, wherein the bat and ball are moving in precisely opposite directions before and after the

FIGURE 47. *Batted-ball speed as a function of the point of impact for a wooden bat and an aluminum bat. The effective hitting surface is larger and closer to the handle of the aluminum bat. [Adapted from P. Brancazio paper presented at the New England section of the American Physical Society Meeting, October 1987.]*

collision. Motion occurs in only one direction. We now wish to generalize our discussion to include the possibility that the bat strikes the ball obliquely, as shown in Figure 48. We again treat the bat as a cylinder whose axis is perpendicular to the path of the ball, but this time the collision might take place as a glancing blow. In addition, we allow for the possibility that the baseball might be rotating before it strikes the bat, and will almost certainly be rotating afterwards. The theory of oblique collisions is complicated, and we will not go into its details,

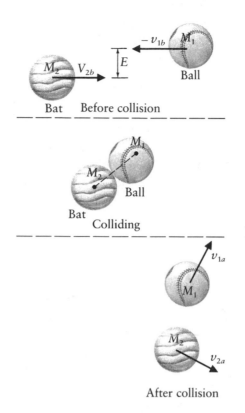

FIGURE 48. *A ball and bat involved in an oblique collision.*

which may be found in Goldsmith.[14] Even in a simple treatment of oblique collisions, however, we must deal with the possibility that the surface of the ball might slip relative to the wooden surface of the bat. We therefore introduce a new property, the coefficient of friction.

Imagine a block resting on a flat surface. If both the surface and the block are perfectly smooth as for an ice cube on a glass table top, the tiniest sideways force will cause the block to slide across the surface (recall Figure 14). For real surfaces, there is always a frictional force that must be overcome before the block will slide (recall Figure 15). This force is equal to the coefficient of friction μ times the weight of the block:

$$\text{Force} = \mu \times \text{weight}$$

If the block is pushed sideways with a force smaller than this value, it will not move. If it is pushed with a larger force, it will slide along the surface.

When a baseball collides with a bat obliquely, there is a force on the ball whose direction goes along a line connecting the centers of the bat and the ball. This is the force that, acting through the coefficient of restitution, causes the ball to bounce off the bat. It also acts like the weight force in the equation for the coefficient of friction. There is, in addition, a force on the ball perpendicular to the line connecting the bat and ball centers. It results from the frictional force between the bat and the ball as they tend to slide past one another. If the ball strikes the bat head on, the frictional force will be zero. As the collision becomes more and more oblique, the force along the ball and bat centers becomes smaller and the frictional force becomes larger, imparting a larger and larger spin to the ball as it leaves the bat. Finally, however, the frictional force reaches some maximum value (depending on the coefficient of friction and how hard the ball is hit). When the collision becomes more oblique than this, the ball surface slips relative to the bat surface and the frictional force reaches its maximum value: that given by the immediately preceeding equation.

We have performed calculations when both the bat speed and the pitch speed were 72 mph. This would be a slow pitch by a major leaguer (see Table 1), and a fast swing (see Table 2). Calculations have been made using three values of the coefficient of friction: 0.1, 0.075, and 0.05. Results are shown graphically in Figures 49 and 50, and in Tables 7, 8, and 9 for precollision ball rotation rates of 1900 rpm, 0 rpm, and −1900 rpm, approximately corresponding to the outside ranges for an overhand curve ball (drop), a knuckle ball, and a fastball, as described in Table 1.

To simplify matters somewhat, let's assume the batter swings in such a way that the direction of the bat velocity is precisely opposite the direction of the ball velocity. The geometry of the situations just a moment before the collision and a few moments after the collision are shown in Figure 48. We will call E the *error in the batter's swing* (as shown in Figure 48).

Consider first the curve ball where $\omega = +1900$ rpm. For small values of E, the distance by which the batter undercuts the ball, the ball does not slip relative to the bat and the rotation rate of the ball after the collision, called the *batted-ball rotation rate*, increases with E. If the coefficient of friction is 0.1, the ball surface does not slip relative to the

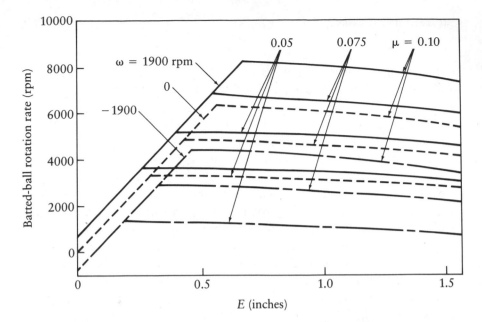

FIGURE 49. *The batted-ball rotation rate as a function of* E, *the distance between the velocity vector of the center of the bat and the velocity vector of the center of the ball as shown in Figure 48.*

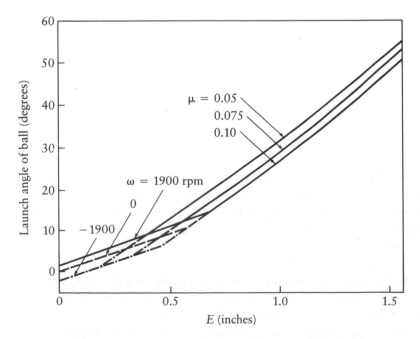

FIGURE 50. *The launch angle of the ball as a function of the batter's error,* E.

μ	E *(in)*	v *(mph)*	Launch Angle θ *(deg)*	ω *(rpm)*
			TABLE 7 Collision Results for 1900-rpm Precollision Rotation Rate	
0.1	0	124	1.9	700
	.2	124	5.4	2800
	.4	123	9.0	4800
	.6	121	12.8	6900
	.7*	120	15.0	7900
	.8	119	18.2	7850
	1.2	114	33.6	7500
0.075	0	124	1.9	700
	.2	124	5.4	2800
	.4	123	9.0	4800
	.55*	122	12.0	6470
	.8	119	20.6	6370
0.05	0	124	1.9	700
	.2	124	5.4	2800
	.43*	123	10.2	4980
	.8	120	23.0	4880

*Slip occurs at larger E.

bat until E reaches 0.7 inch, at which point the ball leaves the bat with a spin rate of 7900 rpm at a launch angle 15 degrees above horizontal. The batted-ball speed is 120 mph, only slightly smaller than the value when $E = 0$, which is 124 mph. Undercutting the ball by a greater amount leads to slip between the ball and bat surfaces. However, even then, both batted-ball speed and rotation rate decrease only very slowly. At $E = 1.0$ inch, the batted-ball rotation rate is 7677 rpm, the speed is 116 mph, and the launch angle is 26.5 degrees.

For the fastball ($\omega = -1900$ rpm), the maximum batted-ball rotation rate when $\mu = 0.1$ is 4190 rpm at $E = 0.46$ inch. The batted-ball speed is 123 mph at a launch angle of 6.6 degrees. If $E = 1$ inch, the speed has decreased to 116 mph, the spin rate is 3858 rpm, and the launch angle is 26.5 degrees.

When the coefficient of friction is lower, the critical value of E is reached sooner. For cases when slip occurs, the rotation rates are lower

μ	E (inches)	v (mph)	Launch Angle (deg)	ω (rpm)
\multicolumn{5}{l}{TABLE 8 Collision Results for −1900-rpm Precollision Rotation Rate}

μ	E (inches)	v (mph)	Launch Angle (deg)	ω (rpm)
0.1	0	124	−1.9	−700
	.2	124	1.7	1380
	.4	123	5.2	3460
	.46*	123	6.6	4190
	.8	119	18.2	4040
0.075	0	124	−1.9	−700
	.2	124	1.7	1380
	.32*	124	3.8	2630
	.4	123	6.4	2700
	.8	119	20.6	2550
	1.2	115	35.9	2300
0.05	0	124	−1.9	−700
	.18*	124	1.4	1180
	.4	123	8.85	1160
	.8	119	23.0	1060

*Slip occurs at larger E.

and the launch angles are larger. Postcollision ball speeds are hardly affected.

There are important lessons to be learned here. When the batter undercuts the ball, even by as much as an inch, very little of the batted-ball speed is lost. The ball can attain a large backspin, even if the ball and bat surfaces slip relative to one another. The launch angle increases at a moderate rate until the ball and bat surfaces slip relative to one another, after which it increases very rapidly. High launch angles, of course, mean pop-ups or foul-backs.

Apparently, the batter has more margin for error than conventional wisdom implies. Undercutting the ball by one half to three quarters of an inch gives the ball backspin while hardly sacrificing batted-ball speed and without popping the ball up. Keep in mind that Steve Garvey said the ball carries better if you undercut it a little (as mentioned in the last paragraph of Chapter 4). Evidently he knows what we have just proved. In the next chapter we study the motions of batted balls after they leave the bat, and show how much farther the ball goes if it has backspin.

μ	E (in)	v (mph)	Launch Angle (deg)	ω (rpm)
0.1	0	124	0	0
	.2	124	3.5	2090
	.4	123	7.1	4160
	.6*	121	11.0	6060
	.8	119	18.2	5950
	1.2	114	33.6	5620
0.075	0	124	0	0
	.2	124	3.5	2090
	.4	123	7.1	4160
	.43*	123	7.9	4560
	.8	119	20.6	4460
	1.2	115	35.9	4210
0.05	0	124	0	0
	.2	124	3.5	2090
	.29*	123	5.3	3080
	.4	123	8.8	3070
	.8	120	23.0	2970

TABLE 9 Collision Results for 0-rpm Precollision Rotation Rate

*Slip occurs at larger E.

Notes

1. Paul Kirkpatrick, "Batting the Ball," *Amer. J. Physics*, vol. 31, 1963, pp. 606–613. A theoretical physics analysis of bat-ball collisions.

2. P. Brancazio, "Swinging for the Fences: The Physics of the Baseball Bat," paper presented at the New England section of the American Physical Society meeting, October 1987. The physics of bat-ball collisions.

3. Tom Meany, "Why So Many Home Runs — Is It $E = 1/2\, mV^2$?," *Collier's*, September 28, 1956.

4. Dan Gutman, "The Physics of Foul Play," *Discover*, April 1988, pp. 70–79. A light treatment of some things baseball players have done to their bats.

5. A. T. Bahill and W. J. Karnavas, "Determining Ideal Baseball Bat Weights Using Muscle Force–Velocity Relationships," *Biological Cybernetics*, vol. 62, 1989, pp. 89–97. The original ideal bat weight study.

6. J. Kaat, "Foul Ball," *Popular Mechanics*, vols. 142 and 145, May 1988, pp. 82–85. Illustrations of some naughty things baseball players have done to their bats.

7. W. O. Fenn and B. S. Marsh, "Muscular Force at Different Speeds of Shortening," *J. Physiol*, vol. 85, 1935, pp. 277–297. A classic paper on the muscle force-velocity relationship.

8. A. V. Hill, "The Heat of Shortening and Dynamic Constraints of Muscle," *Proc. Royal Soc., London, (ser. B)*, vol. 126, 1938, pp. 136–195. Original derivation of the Hill equation for the nonlinear force-velocity relationship of muscle.

9. D. R. Wilke, "The Relation Between Force and Velocity in Human Muscle," *J. Physiol.*, vol. 110, 1950, pp. 249–280. A careful study of the force-velocity relationship of human muscle.

10. B. R. Jewell and D. R. Wilke, "The Mechanical Properties of Relaxing Muscle, *J. Physiol.*, vol. 152, 1960, pp. 30–47. A study of the muscle force-velocity relationship of nonactivated muscle.

11. G. C. Agarwal and G. L. Gottlieb, "Mathematical Modeling and Simulation of the Postural Control Loop — Part II," *CRC Critical Reviews in Biomedical Engineering*, vol. 11, 1984, pp. 113–154. A review of neuromuscular models.

12. P. Brancazio, "Optimal Bat Weight," *American Scientist*, in press. The physics of bat-ball collisions with suggestions of how the bat could be changed to benefit the batter.

13. H. Brody, "The Sweet Spot of a Baseball Bat," *Amer. J. Physics*, vol. 54, 1986, pp. 640–643.

14. W. Goldsmith, *Impact: The Theory and Physical Behavior of Colliding Solids*. Arnold Publ. Co, London, 1960. How things behave when they collide.

The Flight of the Ball:
The Kinetics of Fly Balls

inetics is the study of
the relation between the forces acting on a body, the mass of the body,
and the resulting motion of the body. We have already done some
kinetics calculations in Chapters 2 and 4. We will now study in somewhat greater detail the motion of a baseball in response to the forces it
normally experiences in flight.

The equation that is central to our study is the quantitative expression
of Newton's second law of motion:

$$ma = F$$

There are a number of forces acting on the ball. Obviously, the force exerted by gravity on the ball (the weight) will pull the ball toward the ground. If the ball is spinning, a "lift" force will be exerted in a direction mutually perpendicular to the path of the ball and the axis of spin, as explained in Chapter 2. In that same chapter we mentioned another force: the "drag" force due to the air rushing past the surface of the ball. As a first approximation, we neglected the effect of the drag force on the path of a pitched ball. This is a fairly good approximation as long as the ball is not in the air for longer than about half a second, as happens for pitched balls. (Even then, certain pitches, notably the knuckle ball, are thought to be affected in an important way by the drag force. We will come back to this later.) Fly balls, which might be airborne for 5 to 10 seconds, are strongly affected by both aerodynamic drag and lift induced by the spin of the ball.

As long as the force on the ball is only that caused by gravity, the ball's path will be described by the parabola, as we discussed in Chapter 2, where we first introduced kinetics. In fact, in that chapter we computed the range R of a ball, or the distance a ball will travel when thrown or batted with given initial velocity. The range is given by the equation

$$R = \frac{2v_{x0}\, v_{z0}}{g}$$

We stated in Chapter 5 that if a ball is to travel far enough to be a home run, it needs to leave the bat at about 110 mph (161 ft/s), and in Table 4 we showed that many members of the San Francisco Giants could produce such batted-ball speeds. The range, as computed from the immediately preceding equation, will be a maximum if the ball is hit at a 45 degree angle from the horizontal. In this case the initial velocities v_{x0} and v_{z0} are both 114 feet per second. (Note that $\sqrt{v_{x0}^2 + v_{z0}^2} = 161$ ft/s.) The maximum range is

$$R_{max} = \frac{2\,(114)\,(114)}{32} = 812 \text{ ft}$$

It is improbable that anyone has hit a baseball this far.

The trouble with the above calculation is that we assumed that gravity was the only force acting on the ball. In truth, both aerodynamic drag and lift exert quite large forces. We have already discussed the lift force

"HERE — IF YOU'RE SO DAMN SMART, YOU PITCH A FEW INNINGS."

caused by the spin of the ball. We need to discuss the drag force before proceeding to calculate the trajectories of fly balls.

◆ Drag Force: The Drag Coefficient ◆

As in this case of the lift force, the drag force F_D on a spinning ball is best related to other variables through the set of three dimensionless group equations introduced in Chapter 4. These are

$$G_1 = C_D = \frac{2F_D}{\rho A v^2}$$

$$G_2 = SP = \frac{R\omega}{v}$$

$$G_3 = \text{Re} = \frac{2vR}{v}$$

This time, because of the higher velocity, the *drag coefficient* C_D depends on both the spin parameter SP, and G_3, which is called the *Reynolds number* and is written Re. Unfortunately, the variation of C_D with Re is rather complex. Let us examine what is currently known about this variation.

The maximum value of the Reynolds number that we might expect in baseball would correspond to a ball speed of about 110 to 115 mph, say 170 ft/s. The kinematic viscosity v of air at a temperature of 80°F is about 16×10^{-5} ft²/s. Under these conditions, a 2.85-in diameter ball would have a Reynolds number of

$$\text{Re} = \frac{2\,(170)\,(2.85/12)}{16 \times 10^{-5}} = 2.5 \times 10^5$$

Typical Reynolds numbers experienced by baseballs in play are large, with a maximum of around 2.5×10^5. This is just about the range of Reynolds number where a peculiar phenomenon takes place, leading to a very strong and nonlinear variation of C_D with Re.

Figure 51 shows the variation of drag coefficient with Reynolds number for nonspinning spheres as measured by Achenbach.[1] There are several curves, because there is actually another dimensionless group, called the *relative roughness*, that enters the picture. The relative roughness is defined as ϵ/D, where D is the diameter of the sphere and ϵ is the height of the fine grains of sand that were evenly distributed over the surface of the balls to make them rough in experiments leading to Figure 51. The major facts to notice about Figure 51 are that (1) the drag coefficient is nearly constant over a range of Reynolds numbers from about 10^4 to just over 10^5 and (2) after some critical Reynolds number is exceeded, the drag coefficient drops sharply by a factor of 4 or more, and then begins to increase slowly, and (3) the value of the critical Reynolds number depends on the relative roughness.

The sharp drop in the drag coefficient is not difficult to explain. Refer back for a moment to Figure 18. When a fluid flows past a sphere, the boundary layer tends to separate and a wake forms behind the ball. The pressure within the wake region is much lower than the pressure on the forward half of the ball. At high Reynolds numbers it is this pressure difference that accounts for most of the drag force on the ball. We

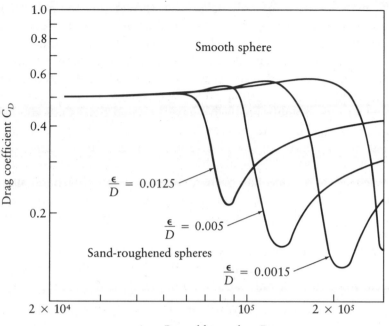

FIGURE 51. *The drag force (as represented here by the dimensionless drag coefficient) is not really constant, but varies with the speed of the ball (as represented here by the dimensionless Reynolds number). For very smooth spheres, it is nearly constant up to speed of about 40 mph, above which it drops off quickly. For sand-roughened spheres, it begins to decrease at much smaller ball speeds, but does not decrease by quite so much. This is why golf balls are made with dimpled surfaces. Spheres with roughened surfaces will fly further than smooth spheres.*

further noted in Chapter 3 that Weisselsberger discovered that by placing a wire around the front part of the sphere one could introduce turbulence into the boundary layer and thereby delay separation and reduce the size of the wake, as shown in the lower picture in Figure 18. Since force is pressure times area, the reduced low pressure wake area reduces the drag force.

What Figure 51 tells us is that the boundary layer will become turbulent if the Reynolds number is made large enough. The rougher the surface of the sphere, the lower the Reynolds number at which the drag coefficient drops.

The manufacturers of golf balls have known this for a long time. Many years ago, when golf balls were smooth, astute golfers noticed that old balls with cut and marred surfaces could be driven much further than the new, smooth balls. At first, balls with bumps distributed on the surface were introduced. These tended to get dirty and to retain lumps of mud. The present day dimpled-surface balls were then introduced.

Some writers (notably Frohlich[2]) have assumed that, since the height of the stitches above the surface of a baseball is about 0.5 mm, the baseball behaves more or less like a rough sphere with a relative roughness of about 0.007. While few drag force measurements are available for baseballs, and none has been reported for spinning baseballs, the available data do not appear to indicate that a baseball behaves like the sand-roughened sphere used in Achenbach's experiments. Figure 52 shows some drag coefficient data reported by Gonzalez[3] along with some golf ball data reported by Bearman and Harvey.[4] Gonzalez used nonspinning baseballs, and the limitations on the wind tunnel used, allowed velocities of only about 75 mph. The huge drops in drag

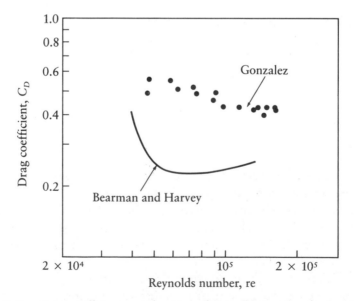

FIGURE 52. *Drag coefficient as a function of Reynolds number for baseballs and golf balls. (Data collected by Richard Gonzalez at Tulane University, and Bearman and Harvey of Imperial College.)*

coefficient experienced by sand-roughened spheres do not appear to be present. However, Hollenberg,[5] also studying nonspinning balls, found fairly large drops in drag coefficient at speeds between 50 and 80 mph for some orientations of the baseball.

The upshot of all this is that we simply do not know how the drag force on a spinning baseball varies with speed. Based on the data of Gonzalez and Hollenberg, we can guess that the drag coefficient decreases with increasing speed, but probably not nearly as rapidly as it does for the smooth or sand-roughened spheres studied by Achenbach. We would guess that the decrease is from about 0.6 to 0.4 over the range of Reynolds numbers typical of baseballs in play. (We note that things might be quite different for spinning balls.) We will make our trajectory calculations based on an assumed constant drag coefficient with a value of 0.5, cautioning the reader that this may be a crude approximation. *Comparative values* of the distance traveled by the ball under a variety of conditions should be reasonably representative of a real-life situation. Frohlich has performed some calculations of the distance traveled by balls with drag coefficients varying as in sand-roughened spheres. He did not, however, account for the lift force caused by spin. In this chapter, we wish to study this effect. The results that we will present have been published by Watts and Baroni[6] and you may consult this paper for details.

◆ *Trajectories* ◆

Determining the path of a ball with Newton's second law generally requires the use of a computer. We will describe the technique briefly and then present some results graphically in Figure 53. At some instant the ball is located at a point (x, z) and is moving with velocity (v_x, v_z). Let F_{Dx} and F_{Dz} be the drag force components in the x and z directions. Similarly, F_{Lx} and F_{Lz} are the lift force components. The quantity v is the speed, which is equal to $\sqrt{v_x^2 + v_z^2}$. Newton's second law yields two equations, one for the x-direction acceleration and one for the z-direction acceleration:

$$ma_x = F_{Dx} - F_{Lx}$$
$$ma_z = -mg - F_{Dz} + F_{Lz}$$

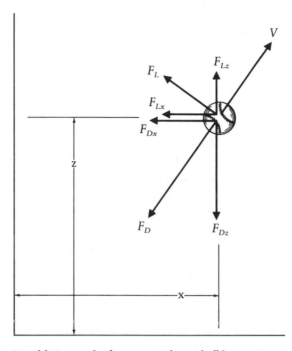

FIGURE 53. *In addition to the force exerted on a ball by gravity, a real ball in flight is subject to at least two other forces, the aerodynamic drag force in a direction opposite the direction of motion, and the lift force, mutually perpendicular to the direction of motion and the spin axis. In this figure (as well as the analysis in the text), we assume the spin axis of the ball is directed into the page. The x- and z-direction forces are obtained by resolving the lift and drag force into the upward and horizontal components.*

If the speed v of the ball and its rotation rate are known, F_D and F_L can be calculated from

$$F_L = \frac{1}{2}\, \rho v^2 \pi R^2 C_L$$

and

$$F_D = \frac{1}{2}\, \rho v^2 \pi R^2 C_D$$

If v_x and v_z are known, the components of F_D and F_L can be determined from similar triangles:

$$\frac{v_x}{v} = \frac{F_{Dx}}{F_D} = \frac{F_{Lz}}{F_L}$$

and

$$\frac{v_z}{v} = \frac{F_{Dz}}{F_D} = \frac{F_{Lx}}{F_L}$$

We can solve the equations sequentially in the following way:

1. Suppose we know the values of v_x and v_z at time $t = 0$, v_{x_0} and v_{z_0}.
2. Using these velocities we calculate all the terms on the right side of the equations.

$$ma_x = F_{Dx} - F_{Lx}$$
$$ma_z = -mg - F_{Dz} + F_{Lz}$$

3. Divide by the mass of the ball to obtain the acceleration terms a_x and a_z.
4. Acceleration is the rate of velocity change with respect to time: $a_x = (v_x - v_{x_0})/\Delta t$ and $a_z = (v_z - v_{z_0})/\Delta t$, where Δt is the change in time. In truth, this formula for acceleration gives the *average* acceleration over the time increment. If you make even a small error, there is sometimes enough difference between the average and instantaneous acceleration values to screw up the trajectory calculations. For you mathematics whizzes, we have used a third-order Runge-Kutta formulation in our numerical calculations. The current description gives the general idea though.
5. Now we know the new velocity components, so we can start from there and repeat things from Step 1. Meanwhile, the distance the ball traveled during the first Δt was

$$\Delta x = \frac{1}{2} (v_x + v_{x_0}) \Delta t$$
$$\Delta z = \frac{1}{2} (v_z + v_{z_0}) \Delta t$$

The trajectory equations were solved initially using time steps of 0.0003 and 0.03 s. An initial ball speed of 110 mph was used in all calculations.

Typically, the difference in ranges was about 2 ft, the smaller time increments giving the longer, more accurate ranges. Some typical trajectories are shown in Figure 54. The dashed line shows the path of a ball with no lift or drag forces at all. Other curves show paths with no lift, but realistic drag force, with topspin of 4000 rpm, and with backspins of 4000 rpm and 6000 rpm. In all cases the launch angle is 30 degrees above the horizontal and the initial speed is 110 mph. Without drag, the ball would travel 700 feet! Note that you can calculate this for yourself using the equation.

$$R = \frac{2v_{x0}\, v_{z0}}{g}$$

The drag force has a large effect. When the drag force, but not the lift force, is included, the ball goes only about half as far. With 4000-rpm backspin, the resulting lift on the ball keeps it in the air longer, and it travels 400 feet! If it were possible to hit a ball with a launch angle of 30 degrees and with 6000 rpm backspin, it would eventually rise at such a steep angle that the lift force would prevent its forward motion and it would travel just over 300 feet. Conversely, topspin leads to a sinking line drive. More general results are shown plotted in Figures 55, 56, and 57. We have used time increments of 0.03 seconds in the calculations.

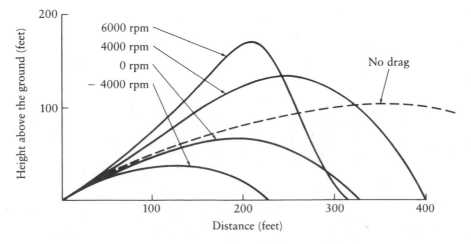

FIGURE 54. *Typical trajectories of batted balls. The ball speed leaving the bat is 110 mph, and the launch angle is 30 degrees above the horizontal.*

FIGURE 55. · *This figure shows how the range of a batted baseball is affected by the spin rate and the launch angle. The speed of the ball leaving the bat is assumed to be 110 mph. To find the range of a particular ball, locate the launch angle on the horizontal axis. Trace upward along a vertical line until you reach a curve labeled with the spin rate of the ball. Then trace along a horizontal line until you reach the vertical axis on the left and read the range.*

First consider Figure 55. When the spin rate on the ball is 0, there is no lift force. The maximum range is about 335 feet. These numbers are similar to those of Frohlich[2] and Brancazio.[7] As the spin rate increases, the maximum range increases dramatically, and occurs at smaller launch angles. When the spin rate is 4000 rpm, the maximum range is 430 ft and the optimum launch angle is 18 degrees.

The data are displayed in a different manner in Figure 56. For a launch angle of 40 degrees the spin rate giving the maximum range (361 ft) is 2300 rpm. If the launch angle is 20 degrees, a maximum range of 440 ft is reached with an optimum spin rate of 4780 rpm.

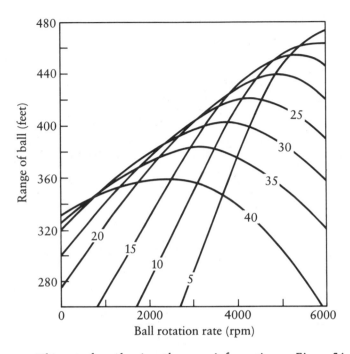

FIGURE 56. *This set of graphs gives the same information as Figure 54. Read in the rotation rate of the ball along the horizontal axis and trace vertically upward to the curve giving the appropriate launch angle. From this point, trace a horizontal line to the vertical axis and read the range.*

To plan an optimum strategy, the analytically inclined batter should study Figure 57. Curves of constant range are there plotted against rotation rate and launch angle. Clearly, the best strategy is to obtain a high backspin rate on the ball at a low launch angle. The *combination* is important. Suppose, for example, that a batter launched a ball optimally just under 40 degrees with a spin rate of 0. The ball would travel 335 ft. If he launched the ball at 39 degrees with a spin rate of 4100 rpm, the range would again be 335 ft. However, if he attained a spin rate of 4100 rpm and launched the ball at the optimum angle of 16 degrees, the range would be 436 ft, 101 ft farther than the nonspinning ball.

These are spectacular numbers. Baseball is supposed to be a game of inches, not tens to hundreds of feet. A central question must be: "How much backspin can one hope to attain while hitting a baseball without fouling the ball back?" This question, of course, forces us to return our attention to the collision calculation. A typical rotation rate of a very

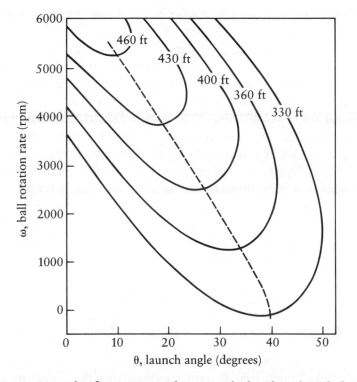

FIGURE 57. *From this figure, we can determine the best launch angle for a given ball backspin rate. The lines of constant range are like the contour lines on the map of a hill. The height of the hill (or the range of the ball) increases as you go towards the upper left-hand corner of the figure. The dashed line is like a ridge on the hill. Suppose a ball is launched with zero backspin. Start at $\omega = 0$ and trace across to the dashed line. The ball should be launched 40 degrees above the horizontal and its range will be a little more than 330 ft. If the batter can manage to put 3000 rpm backspin on the ball, it should be launched at an angle of about 23 degrees above the horizontal, and its range would be about 410 ft.*

good curve ball is about 2000 rpm. It is a little difficult to believe that a batter could produce a rotation rate of 8000 rpm on a fly ball, as is implied by our calculations for the case of a batter undercutting a curve ball by between 0.67 and 1 in when the coefficient of friction is 0.1. It is also difficult to believe that the coefficient of friction between a cowhide sphere and a wooden cylinder is much smaller than 0.1. The coefficient of friction between two billiard balls has been reported as 0.04 by Muller.[8] It is possible, of course, that very large rotation rates can be imparted to baseballs. As far as we know, there have been no rotation rate measurements of batted balls reported in the literature.

There are many potential problems in our collision analysis that are perhaps not made clear enough in the textbooks to students of physics. The classical theory of collision, which we used in our calculations, is called *stereomechanics* (Goldsmith[9]). It is based primarily on the laws of momentum for *rigid* bodies. The theory fails to account for local deformations at the contact point, and further assumes constant values for the coefficients of restitution and friction. The law of conservation of momentum must, of course, not be violated. It is probably the assumptions involving constant coefficients of restitution and friction that lead to problems. On the other hand, perhaps our striking predictions are good approximations of what happens in the real world. Obviously, a controlled experiment is in order. We wish we had the facilities to do such an experiment.

◆ *Some Tentative Conclusions About Hitting* ◆

The *qualitative* conclusion that one reaches from the trajectory calculations are unequivocal. To achieve maximum range, the backspin rate should be high and the launch angle should decrease as the spin rate increases. The effect of increasing the backspin rate is large. A modest backspin rate of 2000 rpm produces an increase in range of about 50 ft (when hit at an optimum launch angle) over that of a nonspinning ball.

Let us assume that the collision calculations in Chapter 5 are accurate in form and orders of magnitude. They imply that a batter should undercut the ball by 0.5 to 1 in. When the ball is undercut by more than this, little of the ball velocity or spin rate is lost, at least until the distance the ball is undercut (E) is greater than about 1.5 inches. The launch angle increases rapidly, however, and the advantage of having a large lift force due to large backspin is lost after about $E = 1$ in. Many writers in the past have suggested that hitting a baseball successfully is so difficult because the margin for error is so small. Conventional wisdom has it that an error in E of only 1 to 2 mm can mean the difference between a home run and a pop fly. Our calculations imply that this is not true. We show this with a possible scenario.

When a overhand curve ball crosses home plate, it is moving slightly downward at an angle of perhaps 10 degrees from the horizontal.

Assume that the batter swings slightly upward at the same angle. If he hits the ball flush ($E = 0$), and he has a bat speed of 60 mph, then from Figure 40, he will produce a batted-ball speed of 110 mph and the result will be a line drive. However, if he undercuts the ball by $1/4$ in, the launch angle would be 5 degrees + 10 degrees = 15 degrees; the batted-ball speed would still be 110 mph, but this time the spin rate would be 2800 rpm. According to Figure 56 this ball would travel about 380 ft. An undercut of $1/2$ in would send the ball about 440 ft, provided the coefficient of friction $\mu \geq 0.05$, while undercutting by $3/4$ in would result in a 390-ft fly, if $\mu \geq 0.075$. When $E = 1/2$ in, approximately optimum conditions are produced, but changing E by a millimeter still produces a long hit. It might be argued, however, that a difference of $1/4$ to $3/4$ in reduces the distance by a substantial 50 ft. The point we wish to make is that the ball has been hit solidly in each of the cases.

The final point we wish to make concerns the importance of the friction coefficient. Figure 49 implies that it is difficult to put large backspin on a fastball unless the coefficient of friction is reasonably large. Note also that a fastball should be undercut by a larger amount than a curve ball, provided the friction coefficient can be made reasonably high. There are many ways to accomplish this. Hitters have been known to carve grooves in their bats, and George Brett of the Kansas City baseball team once had a home run called back because his bat had pine tar on it beyond the "legal" limit — 18 in of handle. The American League president reinstated the home run later and stated that the rule was merely meant to keep the ball clean. We suspect George Brett knew perfectly well what he was doing.

◆ *Home Run Hitting and the Weather* ◆

The year 1987 seems to have been a banner year for home run hitting. As we mentioned in Chapter 5, it is not likely that this increase was caused by an increase in the coefficient of restitution of the ball.

Recently several players have claimed that the Spring and Summer of 1987 were unusually hot and humid and that under these weather conditions the ball goes further. Increasing either the air temperature or humidity would have the effect of lowering the density of the air. This would in turn lower both the drag force and the lift force. While we do not intend to examine this question fully, we will present a few examples with the intention of determining the order of magnitude of the possible effect of weather on the range of batted balls.

We assume the air pressure is 14.7 pounds per square inch, which is normal atmospheric pressure at sea level. If the temperature is 50°F and the humidity is 0, the air density, computed from the ideal gas law, is 0.0779 pound per cubic foot. On the other hand, the density of 90°F air at 100% relative humidity is 0.0709 pound per cubic foot, a decrease of about 9 percent. This is an extreme case of density variation. We decreased the density term in the equations

$$F_L = \tfrac{1}{2}\, \rho v^2 \pi R^2 C_L$$
$$F_D = \tfrac{1}{2}\, \rho v^2 \pi R^2 C_D$$

by 10 percent and recomputed a few of the trajectories. The results are shown in Table 10. The launch angle is θ; the other terms are obvious. The first two rows keep the spin rate and launch angle constant, and vary the air density between its extremes. The last two rows keep the spin rate and launch angle constant at different values, while once again varying the air density between its extremes. Both pairs show that a 10 percent decrease in air density produces a 5 percent increase in how far the ball goes.

The decrease in air density decreases both the drag and the lift forces. Evidently, the decreased drag has the more important effect. A 10 percent decrease in air density causes the ball to travel 20 to 25 feet farther. This is, of course, a very large decrease in air density, and reflects extreme differences in atmospheric conditions. Nevertheless, the results show that temperature and humidity can potentially play an important role in home run hitting.

TABLE 10

ω (rpm)	θ (deg)	T (°F)	Hum (%)	Range (ft)
2865	35	50	0	383
2865	35	90	100	403
4775	20	50	0	439
4775	20	90	100	465

In summary, on a hot, humid day air density is smaller than on a cold, dry day. This allows the ball to travel 5 percent farther. Temperature and humidity also effect the *ball*. Balls stored in 100 percent humidity absorb water, become heavier, have lower coefficients of restitution and subsequently fall somewhat short of balls stored in a normal environment. Conversely, balls stored in a freezer also have lower coefficients of restitution for as long as the center is frozen and fall short of balls at ambient temperature. Unless we know all the details, we should be careful in making generalizations about how the weather effects how far the ball goes.

Notes

1. E. Achenbach, "The Effect of Surface Roughness and Tunnel Blockage in the Flow Past Spheres," *J. Fluid Mech.*, vol. 65, 1977. Drag forces on spheres.

2. C. Frohlich, "Aerodynamic Drag Crisis and Its Possible Effect on the Flight of Baseballs," *Am. J. Physics*, vol. 52, April 1984. How the roughness of a baseball might affect how far it can be hit.

3. R. Gonzalez, *Aerodynamics of a Knuckleball*, honors thesis in mechanical engineering, Tulane University, 1968. Wind tunnel measurements of the forces on the knuckleball.

4. P. W. Bearman and J. K. Harvey, "Golf Ball Aerodynamics," *Aeronauts Quarterly*, vol. 27, 1976, p. 112. Drag and lift forces on spinning golf balls by some British scientists.

5. J. W. Hollenberg, "Secrets of the Knuckleball," *The Bent of Tau Beta Pi*, series 4, vol. 77, 1986, pp. 26–30. More measurements, and computer predictions of the path of the knuckleball.

6. R. G. Watts and S. Baroni, "Baseball-Bat Collisions and the Resulting Trajectories of Spinning Balls, *Am. J. Physics*, vol. 57, Jan. 1989. How spin affects how far a baseball can be hit.

7. P. Brancazio, *SportScience: Physical Laws and Optimum Performance*, Simon and Schuster, New York, 1984. A great book on the physics of all sports. A must for scientific sports fans.

8. W. Muller, *Ost. Ing. Arch.*, vol. 6, 1952. More about collisions.

9. W. Goldsmith, *Impact: The Theory and Physical Behavior of Colliding Solids*, Arnold Publ. Co, London, 1960. How things behave when they collide.

Baseball Players Cannot Keep

Their Eyes on the Ball

ed Williams, arguably the best hitter in the history of baseball, has described hitting a baseball as the most difficult single act in all of sports.[2] The velocity of a pitch approaches 100 mph. Tracking such a ball as it crossed the plate would require head and eye rotations in excess of 1000 degrees per second: a century of scientific literature says that humans cannot track targets moving faster than 90 degrees per second. Yet, major league

---

This chapter is based on the work of Bahill and LaRitz.[1] (1984).

batters manage to hit the ball with force consistently, and are able to "get a piece of the ball" in 80 percent of their swings.[3] In this chapter we investigate how they do this by examining the head and eye movements of a professional athlete tracking a pitched ball, and we demonstrate the superiority of his eye movements and head-eye coordination to those of college athletes.

We studied our batters' use of the four basic types of eye movements: *saccadic eye movements*, which are used in reading text or scanning a room; *smooth pursuit eye movements,* used when tracking a moving object; *vergence eye movements,* used when looking between near and far objects; and *vestibulo-ocular eye movements,* used to maintain fixation during head movements. These four types of eye movements have independent control systems, involving different areas of the brain. Their dynamic properties, such as latency (the time between the target movement and the beginning of the eye movement) and speed are different, and they are affected differently by fatigue, drugs, and disease.

The specific actions of these four systems can be illustrated by the example of a duck hunter sitting in a rowboat on a lake. He scans the sky using saccadic eye movements, jerking his eyes quickly from one fixation point to the next, so as to place his fovea (the small area in the center of the retina that has excellent acuity) on the area of interest. When he spots a duck, he tracks it using smooth pursuit eye movements. If the duck comes close to him, he tracks it by moving his eyes toward each other with vergence eye movements. Throughout all this, he uses vestibulo-ocular eye movements to compensate for the movement of his head caused by the rocking of the boat. Thus, all four systems are continually used to move the eyes.

In addition to each of these eye-movement systems, the batter has the potential to use the head-movement system. Earlier studies suggested three increasingly more complex strategies for tracking the baseball: track the ball with only eye movements, and fall behind in the last 10 ft; track the ball with head movements and smooth pursuit eye movements and fall behind in the last 5 ft; track the ball over the first part of its trajectory with smooth pursuit eye movements, make a saccadic eye movement to a predicted point ahead of the ball, continue to follow it with peripheral vision, and finally, at the end of the ball's flight, resume smooth pursuit tracking with the ball's image on the fovea. We will examine each of these strategies.

◆ *The Simulated Fastball* ◆

To discover how well a batter tracked the ball, we had to be able to determine the position of the ball at all times. If we had used a human pitcher or a throwing machine, we would have had to use radar or high-speed photography to measure the position of the ball. We thought this would be too complicated. Instead, we simulated the trajectory of a pitched baseball. (See Figure 58.) We threaded a fishing line through a white plastic ball and stretched this line between two supports, which were set 80 ft apart in order to comfortably accommodate the 60.5 ft between the pitcher's rubber and home plate; a string was attached to the ball and wrapped around a pulley attached to a motor, so that when the motor was turned on, the string pulled the ball down the line at speeds between 60 and 100 mph. The ball crossed the plate 30 in away from the subject's shoulders, simulating a high-and-outside fastball thrown by a left-handed pitcher to a right-handed batter. This, like all our contraints, was designed to give our subjects the best possible chance of keeping their eyes on the ball. A low curve ball thrown by a right-handed pitcher would have been much harder to track. Throughout this chapter all our descriptions are for right-handed batters against left-handed pitchers.

By controlling the speed of the motor (which was actually a $15,000 velocity servo system) and counting the rotations of the shaft, we could compute the position of the ball at every instant of time, and thus compare the position of the ball to the position of the batter's gaze. We define both positions in terms of the horizontal angle of the ball: the angle between the line of sight pointing at the ball and a line perpendicular to the subject's body. (See Figure 59.) This angle is about 0 degrees when the pitcher releases the ball, and it increases to 90 degrees when the ball crosses the plate.

We monitored horizontal eye movements with a photoelectric system using infrared emitters and photodetectors mounted on spectacle frames (as shown in Figure 58) and aimed at the sides of the blue or brown irises.[4] As the eye moved horizontally, the amount of reflected infrared light changed, causing a variation in the current of the photodetectors. Amplifying the difference in the currents of the two detectors produced a voltage proportional to horizontal eye position. Although we sampled each millisecond, our data were filtered and compressed to produce position traces with a bandwidth of 30 Hz and velocity traces with a bandwidth of 7 Hz. Since we deliberately configured the experi-

FIGURE 58. *Our simulated fastball was produced when the white plastic ball was pulled along the fishing line by the string, which was connected to a motor. The infrared emitters and photodetectors that monitored the eye movements of a subject trying to track this ball were mounted on the special eye glasses shown here worn by Dr. Bahill. Two light-emitting diodes used to monitor head movements sit directly on top of the head, and the third is at the end of the stalk.*

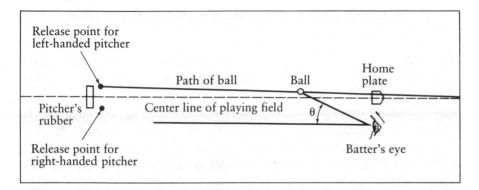

FIGURE 59. *The horizontal angle of the ball, θ, as defined in this study, ranges from near 0 degrees when the pitcher releases the ball, to 90 degrees when the ball crosses the plate. [From A. T. Bahill and T. LaRitz, American Scientist, 72:249–253, 1984.]*

ment to minimize vertical target movements, vertical eye movements, which were measured with electro-oculography but are not shown in our figures, were negligibly small.

Head movements were monitored with a TV camera mounted on the ceiling, looking down on the subject's head. Two light-emitting diodes (LEDs) were placed on top of the subject's head, and a third LED was mounted on a stalk 7.8 in above the head as shown in Figure 58. The camera's signal was digitized and stored in a computer. The coordinates of the centers of the three LEDs were computed, and from these we computed the yaw, pitch, and roll angles, as well as the lateral and forward-backward translations of the head.

Yaw is rotation about the vertical axis, as occurs when shaking your head when answering no to a question. Pitch is rotation about a horizontal axis (specifically the y axis of Figure 10 in Chapter 2), as occurs when shaking your head when answering yes to a question. When a ship alternately dips its bow and stern it is said to be pitching. Roll is rotation about a different horizontal axis (specifically the x axis of Figure 9 in Chapter 2), as occurs when cocking your head. When a ship rocks from side to side it is said to be rolling.

We ran several subjects in our experiment, including graduate students, undergraduate students on the university baseball team, and Brian Harper, then a member of the Pittsburgh Pirates and later a member of the Saint Louis Cardinals, all had 20/20 uncorrected vision.

◆ *Gaze Position While Tracking the Ball* ◆

Figure 60 shows the data of one experiment, which were typical of the results obtained with students. This subject tracked the ball well (less than 2 degrees error) until the ball was 9 ft in front of the plate, then he fell behind. When the ball was 2 ft in front of the plate, the image of the ball was 34 degrees off his fovea. To see what it means for an object to be 34 degrees off your fovea, hold a 1-foot ruler at arm's length. If you look at the left end, the right end will be about 34 degrees off your fovea. While looking at the left end, you will not be able to read the numbers on the right end. The ball covered the distance between 9 ft and 2 ft in front of the plate in 67 millisecond (ms) for an average angular velocity of over 500 degrees per second—much too fast for humans to track. The maximum smooth pursuit velocity occurred just before the ball crossed the plate: the eye was going 50 degrees per second, and the head was going 20 degrees per second, giving a gaze velocity of 70 degrees per second. This subject used primarily eye movements to track the ball; the head movements came too late in the trajectory to be of use in tracking. Other students used only head movements to track the ball. After the ball crossed the plate, this subject (like most of our students) made large head and eye movements.

Figure 61 shows the results produced by the professional ball player Brian Harper while tracking three of our fastballs. Let us look in detail at the second pitch, Figure 61*b*. He tracked the ball using head *and* eye movements, keeping his eye on the ball longer than our other subjects did. He was able to keep his position error below 2 degrees until the ball was 5.5 ft from the plate, at which point he began to fall behind. When the ball was 2 ft in front of the plate the image of the ball was already 16 degrees off his fovea and was going 1,100 degrees per second. Thus he was no longer tracking the ball.

While tracking the ball, as shown in Figure 61*b*, the eye angle changed by 17 degrees and the head horizontal rotation angle (yaw) changed by 13 degrees. Thus he used his head and his eyes to track the ball.*

The peak velocity of his smooth pursuit tracking was 120 degrees per second; at this point his head velocity was 30 degrees per second, thus producing a gaze velocity of 150 degrees per second. In three experi-

---

*Because the movement of the ball was primarily horizontal, the measured head pitch and roll angles changed very little, that is, by less than 2 degrees.

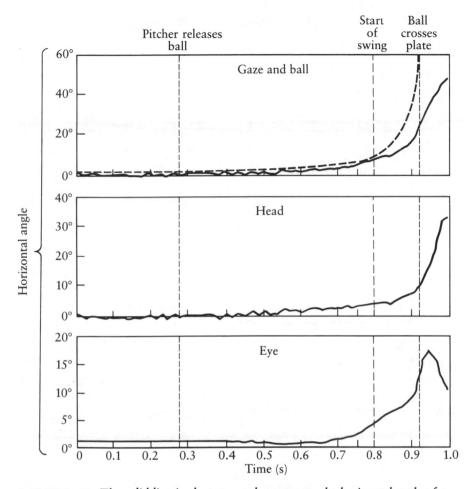

FIGURE 60. *The solid line in the top graph represents the horizontal angle of our experimental 70-mph fastball as it would be seen by a right-handed batter facing a left-handed pitcher; the dashed line represents the horizontal angle of gaze of the subject, a graduate student, trying to track this ball. This gaze graph is generated by combining horizontal head angle (middle graph) and horizontal eye angle (bottom graph). Movements to the right appear as upward deflections. It is the time when the horizontal velocity of the bat toward the ball became greater than zero. There are minor vertical and rotational movements before this. [A. T. Bahill and T. LaRitz, American Scientist, 72:249–253, 1984.]*

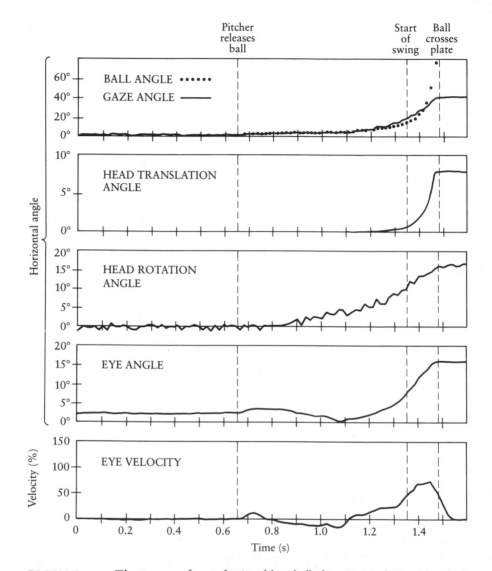

FIGURE 61a. *The success of a professional baseball player in tracking our experimental 60-mph fastball is shown in graphs, which the same format as in Figure 60, except that the horizontal-gaze angle also takes into account the head-translation angle shown in the middle graph, which represents the eye movements necessary to compensate for side-to-side and front-to-back movements of the head.*

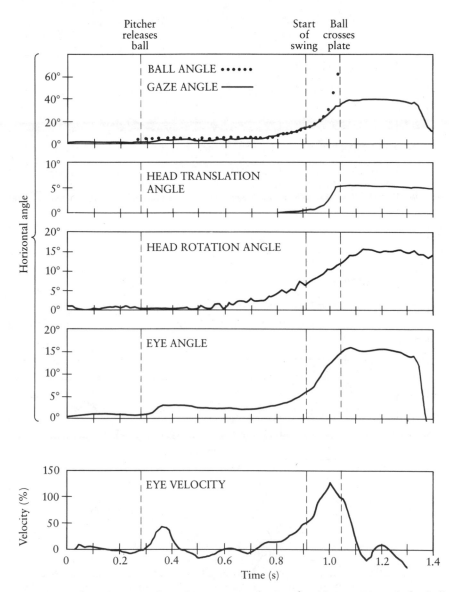

FIGURE 61b. *The second pitch to our professional athlete, a 70-mph fastball. Same format as in Figure 61a. [Adapted from A. T. Bahill and T. LaRitz,* American Scientist, *72:249–253, 1984.]*

FIGURE 61c. *The third pitch to our professional athlete, a 70-mph fastball. Same format as in Figure 61b. The equipment broke at the point indicated by the arrow and the ball began to slow down. However, the subject continued to track as if nothing had happened. This caused his eye to get ahead of the ball.*

mental pitches to the professional athlete, at speeds of 60, 67, and 70 mph, the overall tracking patterns were the same; his maximum smooth pursuit eye velocities were 120, 130, and 120 degrees per second, respectively. These numbers are much faster than those commonly reported in the oculomotor literature. One detail, the small saccade at 0.3 s (which shows up as a small, fast movement in the eye trace and as a hump with a peak value of 50 degrees per second in the eye velocity trace) in Figure 61*b*, does not appear in the other pitches, but it is, we think, insignificant.

Our computer algorithms for producing the gaze graphs of the professional athlete (Figure 61) were more complicated than those used for the gaze graph of the student in Figure 60 in that, in addition to combining eye angle and head angle, they also take into account the side-to-side and front-to-back movements of the head; such translations of the head can produce changes in the gaze angle.[5] The data show that the contribution of this translation angle was slight until the ball was almost over the plate.

We have often heard the batting axiom "Don't move your head." So we thought the vestibulo-ocular system would not be used when tracking a baseball. However, in monitoring the eyes of the professional ball player, we detected a small vestibulo-ocular eye movement to the left during the early part of the ball's trajectory, as the head was moving to the right; this appears as the downward deflection between 0.8 and 1.1 s in the eye trace of Figure 61*a*. At this point the head position was changing faster than the angular position of the ball, and the vestibulo-ocular eye movement compensated for the premature head movement. The batter was apparently giving his head a head start. Why would he want to do this? Because the head is heavier than the eye and consequently takes longer to get moving; therefore, in the beginning of the movement, as the head starts turning to the right (ahead of the ball), the vestibular system in the inner ear signals the oculomotor system to make a compensating leftward eye movement. This allows the head to start turning while the gaze remains fixed on the ball.

However, this vestibulo-ocular compensation must soon stop. In the last half of the ball's flight, the eye and head must both be moving to the right, and the batter must, therefore, suppress his vestibulo-ocular reflex, so that the tracking head movement does not produce compensating eye movements that would take his eye off the ball. The professional athlete was very good at suppressing his vestibulo-ocular reflex. Most of our student subjects tracked the ball with either head movements alone or eye movements alone, but not both. Perhaps they did this because they could not suppress their vestibulo-ocular reflexes as well.

There is one other noteworthy difference between the tracking of the students and the professional athlete. After the ball crossed the plate, the students usually made large eye or head movements, whereas the gaze of the professional athlete was quite steady.

The stance of our professional athlete was very repeatable. At the beginning of the pitch, his head position was the same (within 1 degree) for each of the three experimental pitches we recorded. When he was looking at the ball in the beginning of the experiment, his eyes were rotated 22 degrees to the left; his head was rotated left 65 degrees (yaw), was bowed down 23 degrees (pitch), and was tilted right 12 degrees (roll).

Obviously, the professional athlete had faster smooth pursuit eye movements than our other subjects. In fact, he had faster smooth pursuit eye movements than any reported in the literature. He also had better head-eye coordination, as shown in the region where he was giving his head a head start. In addition, he was better at suppressing the vestibulo-ocular reflex and making his head and eyes move in the same direction. This allowed him to track the ball with equal-sized head and eye movements, whereas the other subjects usually tracked with either head or eye movements. Together these three superiorities allowed the professional athlete to track the ball to 5.5 ft in front of the plate compared to our students who fell behind at the 9-ft mark.

◆ *Limitations* ◆

We caution that our study, although it does warrant some useful generalizations, has limitations. First, our data pool was small. These experiments were difficult to perform, and from our 50 hours of data collection (and thousands of hours setup time and data analysis) we have complete head and eye data for 6 "pitches," and partial data for another 15 — a total of 11 seconds of data. Second, because we were afraid that they would break our equipment, we never let our subjects actually swing the bat at the ball; it is possible that head-eye coordination would be different if the subjects did swing the bat. Third, we produced the easiest pitch for the batter to track: a high-and-outside fastball thrown by an opposite-handed pitcher, in this case a left-handed pitcher to a right-handed batter. Nevertheless, even with these limitations, we can reasonably make some generalizations.

♦ *No One Can Keep His Eye on the Ball* ♦

Although the professional athlete was better than the students at tracking our fastball, it is clear from our experiments that batters, even professional batters, cannot keep their eyes on the ball. Our professional athlete was able to track the ball until it was 5.5 ft in front of the plate. This could hardly be improved on; we hypothesize that the best imaginable athlete could not track the ball closer than 5 ft from the plate, at which point it is moving three times faster than the fastest human could track.

When questioned about our data, several professional baseball players have said things like "I try to watch the ball all the way to the plate, and if I'm hitting well, I do think I can follow it all the way."[6] When asked what the ball looked like at the time of collision, they said "like a ball." When shown the picture of Figure 35 in Chapter 5, they usually responded with "Well, maybe I don't really see the ball hit the bat."

One question we are often asked: "How slow would the ball have to go, so that the batter could keep his eye on the ball?" This question, however, seems to relate to linear velocity, whereas it is the angular velocity that is important. (Angular velocity is the rate of change of the angle θ in Figure 59.) The ball has an almost constant linear velocity as it travels between the pitcher's mound and the plate. But its angular velocity with respect to the batter changes drastically. To illustrate this point, note that it is easy to track for minutes an airplane flying at an altitude of 5000 ft, but it is not possible to track, for even a few seconds, a jet plane flying 100 feet directly overhead. In both cases the airplane may have the same linear velocity, but the angular velocities are drastically different. So the head and eye movements needed to track it are much different. To help answer the question of how slow the ball would have to go to allow tracking, we ran a computer simulation of the batter tracking the ball. Figure 62 shows the results of this simulation. It shows the distance in front of the plate where the eyes would fall behind the ball for different pitch speeds. We were very conservative in determining this distance. We let the computer track up to 300 degrees per second;

AS SMART AS HE WAS, ALBERT EINSTEIN COULD NOT FIGURE OUT HOW TO HANDLE THOSE TRICKY BOUNCES AT THIRD BASE.

which is twice faster than our professional athlete, and three times as fast as any human reported in the oculomotor literature over the last 40 years. No data points are shown at or below 20 mph, because such a pitch would hit the ground before it crossed the plate. According to this equation from Chapter 2

$$R = \frac{2v_{x0}\, v_{z0}}{g}$$

the slowest pitch that could reach the plate would be 21 mph* (assuming no air resistance, and that $v_{x_0} \geq v_{z_0}$; i.e., it was thrown at less than a 45

---

*For the shorter 46-ft distance between the rubber and home plate of Little League and softball, the slowest pitch that could reach the plate would be 18 mph.

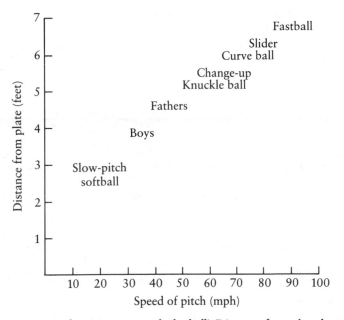

FIGURE 62. *How close can you track the ball? Distance from the plate when the best imaginable athlete could no longer keep his eye on the ball is plotted against the speed of the pitch.*

degree angle). (This assumption is reasonable, because if $v_{x_0} < v_{z_0}$, then you would just loose the ball in the vertical plane before the horizontal plane.) We have also labeled Figure 62 with speed information taken from Table 1 in Chapter 3. It shows, for example, that 7- to 9-year-old boys throw the ball at speeds between 30 and 40 mph. A batter trying to hit a pitch thrown by such a boy would fall behind when the ball was 3 to 4 ft in front of the plate. This leads to the quite astounding conclusion that the batter can't keep his or her eye on the ball even in Little League or slow pitch softball!

◆ *The Alternate Strategy* ◆

This finding, that no athlete could track the ball within 5 ft of the plate, runs contrary to one of the most often repeated axioms of batting instructors: — "Keep your eye on the ball" — and makes it difficult to

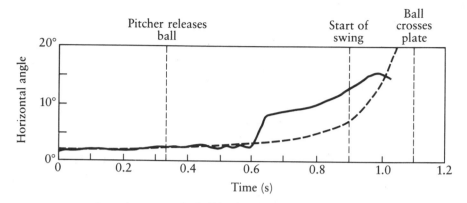

FIGURE 63. *In order to see the ball hit his bat, this subject made an anticipatory saccade, indicated by the jump in the gaze angle (solid line) at 0.6 s, that put his eye ahead of the ball (dashed line); as a result, the ball was on the fovea at the point of contact. The subject did not move his head until after the ball crossed the plate. [From A. T. Bahill and T. LaRitz,* American Scientist, *72:249–253, 1984.]*

account for the widely reported claim that Ted Williams could see the ball hit his bat.

If Ted Williams were indeed able to do this, it could only be possible if he made an anticipatory saccade that put his eye ahead of the ball and then let the ball catch up to his eye. This was the strategy employed by the subject of Figure 63; this batter observed the ball over the first third of its trajectory, predicted where it would be when it crossed the plate, and then made an anticipatory saccade that put his eye ahead of the ball, thereby allowing the ball to catch up to his eye. Using this strategy, the batter could see the ball hit the bat. However, let us note that in a personnel communication Ted Williams said that it was "only on very rare occasions" that he could see the ball hit the bat. It seems that he rarely used this strategy of taking his eye off of the ball, so that he could see it hit his bat.

If a batter does use this strategy, the anticipatory saccade must be made before the end of the ball's trajectory, because saccadic suppression prevents us from seeing during saccades.[7-8] To see the effects of this suppression look at the image of your right eye in a mirror. Now look at the image of your left eye. Did you see your eyes move? Probably not, because we have a process that turns off the visual system during saccadic eye movements. This is a comforting thing to do, because otherwise every time we made a saccadic eye movement, we would think that the world was flying around us. To prevent such confusion we suppress vision during saccades. This suppression of vision exists for about 20 ms before and after the saccade. So if you want to see the ball hit the bat, you must make your anticipatory saccade early in the trajectory. This means that you have to take your eye off the ball at precisely the time when you want to be seeing the ball the best. Using an anticipatory saccade to put your eye ahead of the ball may be an oft-trained strategy, but it is probably not the best strategy for hitting the ball.

Why would a batter on the other hand, want to see the ball hit the bat? He could not, because of his slow reaction time, use the information gained in the last portion of the ball's flight to alter the course of the bat. We suggest that he uses the information to discover the ball's actual trajectory; that is, he uses it to learn how to predict the ball's location when it crosses the plate — how to be a better hitter in the future. The batter says to himself, "I thought the ball was going to be right there. But instead it was a half-inch lower. I will predict better the next time the pitcher throws that pitch." Figure 61c offers further evidence that the batter uses his predictive abilities to help track the ball. At the point indicated by the arrow, our string broke and the ball began to decelerate. But the batter ignored the real world and continued to follow his predictions, which put his eye ahead of the ball.

We have shown that no one could keep his eye continuously on the ball as it flys from the pitcher to the plate. For our professional athlete the ball was always more than 2 degrees off his fovea before it came within 5 ft of the plate. However, when the ball is off your fovea, you can still see with peripheral vision. However, with peripheral vision, the ball would only appear as a white blur; you would not see details. For example, with peripheral vision you could not count the red stitches on the ball, read the label on the bat, or see whether the ball hit the bat in the center or an eighth of an inch below. So we remain confident in our statement that batters cannot keep their eyes on the ball.

It has often been said that athletes are dumb. Our studies have shown the contrary. They are not paid a million dollars for their 6-month job because of their bodies; it's because of their brains. The players that are paid the most have the best brains: they can predict the flight of the pitch better than other mere mortals.

◆ *Other Movement Systems* ◆

Batters do not use vergence eye movements. This is reasonable, since negligibly small vergence eye movements are needed to track the ball between 60 and 6 ft from the plate, and since there is not sufficient time to make such movements between 6 ft and the point of contact; indeed, our data contained no vergence eye movements. So any claim that a batter actually saw the ball hit the bat must be based on monocular vision; only one eye tracks the ball.

The fact that our professional athlete used his head to help track the ball seems to violate another often repeated batting axiom: "Don't move your head." The professional made tracking head movements between 10 and 20 degrees, which were probably small enough to go unnoticed by a coach. What the batter does not want to do is to allow rotations of the body to drag the head along. These body movements could produce head movements of 90 degrees or more, which, along with correlated poor performance, would be noticed by a coach. Therefore, we think the axiom should be protracted: "Don't let your body move your head, but it's okay to move your head to track the ball."

If we can change the subject for a moment from the batter to the umpire, we find some interesting advice in *The Umpire's Handbook*.[9] It says, "The umpire should follow the ball *with his eyes only*." We do not think the authors really meant this, because they follow with phrases like "If he moves his body," and " . . . jerking your head around." I think they meant that it is detrimental to tracking success if body movements are allowed to induce head movements. The data of this chapter indicate that batters and umpires should track the ball normally, that is, with head and eye movements. However, the head movements must be small tracking movements that will not be seen by a faraway observer, not large body-induced head movements.

◆ *Does It Curve or Drop?* ◆

In Chapter 4 we stated that the curve ball can curve horizontally and drop vertically. We explained the advantage of the drop by noting that the sweet spot on the bat is about 6-in long and only half-an-inch high. Thus a drop would be much more effective at taking the ball away from the bat's sweet spot than a curve. However, we have observed a Nolan Ryan curve ball that dropped 2 ft but also curved 2 ft. Why would he want it to curve?

It is well known in baseball that right-handed batters have significantly greater success hitting against left-handed pitchers than against right-handed pitchers. The obverse is true for left-handed batters. This difference in most batters' ability is perplexing, since our computer analysis shows that an overhand fastball thrown by a right-handed pitcher to a right-handed batter would have started with an initial horizontal angle of +1 degree instead of the +3 degrees for a left-handed pitcher; this 2 degree offset in the beginning is completely insignificant. Furthermore, over the last third of the pitch, there is no difference in either angular position or angular velocity. We suspect, with little evidence, that for a right-handed batter, the right-handed pitcher is harder to hit than the left-handed pitcher, only for the curve ball, not for the fastball.

The advantage of the opposite-handed batter is conjectured by Karl Schurr of Bowling Green State University to be nothing more than fear:

> When a right-handed batter sees a ball thrown by a right-handed pitcher coming straight at his head he doesn't know if it is a curve ball that will cross the plate for a strike, or a wild fastball that will hit his head. On the other hand, the left-handed pitcher would have to be wild as a March hare to raise as much adrenaline in the batter.

We conclude therefore that the curve ball should drop as much as possible in order to avoid the bat, but it should also curve to induce fear and confound the batter. We would expect right-handed pitchers to make their curve balls primarily drop when throwing to left-handed batters, and to substitute more horizontal curve when throwing to right-handed batters.

◆ *The Illusion of the Rising Fastball* ◆

At the end of Chapter 4 we applied the principles of physics to the pitched ball and concluded that a rising fastball is unlikely. Yet many batters claim it exists. They say it jumps about a foot right in front of home plate. Let us now apply principles of systems engineering (which

includes aspects of human factors engineering, physiology, and psychology) to explain the rising fastball.

First we show the results of a computer simulation of the fastball. In Figure 64a we show the trajectory of a 95-mph fastball, and the trajectory of a 90-mph fastball. We ignore wind resistance and lift effects due to spin. These simplifications are valid for the comparisons we are going to make. For this simulation the point where the pitcher released the ball was set to be 6 feet high and 55.5 feet in front of the plate. The point where the bat hits the ball was set 1.5 feet in front of the batter's head, which was assumed to be aligned with the front of the plate. These numbers could vary by a half foot for individual players. However, varying them by as much as 3 feet had no effect on our conclusions. The 95-mph pitch was launched at an angle of +0.1 degree (i.e., 0.1 degree up) and the 90-mph pitch was launched horizontally (i.e., zero degrees). For clarity the horizontal and vertical scales are not the same (i.e., 6 feet vertically is about the same as 32 feet horizontally). The slower pitch takes longer to get to the plate and it drops more.

Now, if the batter is to hit the ball, he must predict where it will be when it crosses the plate. We say that he creates a mental model of the pitch. Many times in this chapter we have alluded to the batter's use of mental models to predict the trajectory of the ball. The use of such models in eye tracking is explained in detail by Bahill and McDonald[10,11] (1983a,b) and McDonald and Bahill.[12] Michael McBeath, a professor of psychology at Stanford University, theorizes that the illusion of the rising fastball is the result of the batter's mistake in formulating his mental model. For example, suppose the pitcher threw a 95-mph fastball, but the batter underestimated its speed and thought it was only going 90 mph. He would use his mental model and predict that the ball would cross the plate 3.31 feet above the ground. Now if he were to take his eye off the ball (indicated by the disappearance of some circles

FIGURE 64. (a) *Computer simulation of the trajectory of a 95-mph fastball (solid line and circles) and a 90-mph fastball (dashed line and triangles). The angle labeled θ indicates the direction of motion; (b) the trajectory of a 95-mph fastball (solid line and circles), the batter's mental model of this trajectory (dashed line and triangles) when he underestimated the speed of the pitch by 5 mph, and the batter's line of sight for one of these points (thin dashed line). The angle labeled φ indicates the angle of the batter's line of sight; (c) the same simulation as 64(a) except this time we assumed that when the ball was 20 feet in front of the plate, he realized his internal model was wrong and corrected it, thus putting his mental model triangles on the 95-mph trajectory.*

in Figure 64*b*) in order to see his bat at the expected time of impact, then the next time he saw the ball it would be 3.68 feet above the ground, four inches above his bat. He might explain this by saying, "The ball jumped four inches right in front of the plate." If he underestimated the speed at 81 mph, he would say the ball jumped 1 foot. The manager in the dugout, the catcher, and the center field TV camera, having different perspectives and models, would not see this jump. It is most likely that the batter's perceived jump is the result of his perspective and his underestimation of the speed of the pitch for his mental model.*

However, most batters do not perceive rising fastballs on every pitch. In fact, most of the time batters are able to correct their mental models. How can they tell that their original estimate was wrong? There are three clues they could use: (1) line of sight, (2) direction of motion in depth, and (3) depth perception.† As we show in Table 11, until the ball is within 15 feet of the plate, the differences in the lines of sight to the ball (the thin dashed line in Figure 64b) for the 95-mph pitch and the 90-mph pitch are less than one-half degree. McBeath says these differences are too small for a batter to perceive. So the batter cannot use line of sight information to warn himself of his underestimation of speed in his mental model.

When an object moves directly toward the head, the two retinal images move away from each other and the images also become larger. Using these two primary stimuli for judging motion in depth, half-degree differences in direction can be detected.[13] The 95- and 90-mph fastballs of Figure 64b did not differ in direction by one-half degree until after the ball crossed the plate. So the batter cannot use motion in depth information to warn of his inaccurate mental model.

When two baseballs are mounted 29 and 30 feet from an observer, it is difficult to tell which one is closer. Depth perception for moving balls in sequential trials would be even more difficult. So until the ball is within 20 or 25 feet of the plate, it is unlikely that the batter uses depth perception to warn himself of the error in his mental model.

Let us now reconsider our alternative strategies for tracking the ball. The *optimal learning strategy*, which allows the batter to see the ball hit

---

*In fast-pitch softball the ball really does rise: it is no illusion. A rising fastball in softball is possible because the pitcher's motion is altogether different.

† The batter could also use derivatives of line of sight and direction of motion, but we have no data about human capabilities in manipulating such information.

TABLE 11 Comparison of 95- and 90-mph Fastballs

	95-mph Pitch				90-mph Pitch				Difference		
time (s)	x (ft)	z (ft)	θ (deg)	φ (deg)	x (ft)	z (ft)	θ (deg)	φ (deg)	Δx	Δθ	Δφ
0.000	55.5	6.00	0.1	0.00	55.5	6.00	0.0	0.00	0.0	−0.10	0.00
0.050	48.5	5.97	−0.6	−0.03	48.9	5.96	−0.7	−0.05	0.4	−0.14	−0.02
0.100	41.6	5.86	−1.2	−0.19	42.3	5.84	−1.4	−0.22	0.7	−0.18	−0.03
0.150	34.6	5.67	−1.9	−0.54	35.7	5.64	−2.1	−0.58	1.1	−0.21	−0.04
0.200	27.6	5.41	−2.5	−1.23	29.1	5.36	−2.8	−1.27	1.5	−0.25	−0.04
0.250	20.7	5.06	−3.2	−2.62	22.5	4.99	−3.5	−2.56	1.8	−0.29	0.06
0.300	13.7	4.63	−3.9	−5.73	15.9	4.55	−4.2	−5.20	2.2	−0.32	0.53
0.350	6.7	4.11	−4.5	−15.64	9.3	4.03	−4.9	−11.96	2.6	−0.36	3.68
0.388	1.5	3.68	−5.0	−57.14							
0.400					2.7	3.43	−5.6	−43.63			
0.409					1.5	3.31	−5.7	−60.87			

Notes: x is the distance to the plate.
  z is the height of the ball above the ground.
  θ is the direction of motion of the ball with respect to the horizontal.
  φ is the batter's line of sight to the ball with respect to the horizontal.
  The Δ's are the differences between the 90 and 95 mph pitches.

the bat, is: track the ball over the first part of its trajectory with smooth pursuit eye movements, make a saccadic eye movement to a predicted point ahead of the ball, continue to follow the ball with peripheral vision letting the ball catch up to the eye, and, finally, at the end of the ball's flight, resume smooth pursuit tracking with the images of the ball and bat on the fovea. The *optimal hitting strategy*, which does not allow the batter to see the ball hit the bat; is: track the ball with head movements and smooth pursuit eye movements and fall behind in the last 5 feet. With the optimal learning strategy shown in Figure 64b a batter would perceive many rising fastballs, because his eye would not be on the ball when it was 15 to 25 feet in front of the plate, (which is why we have erased some circles from the plot) and therefore his depth perception and line of sight information could not warn him of an inaccurate model. With the optimal hitting strategy a batter would perceive fewer rising fastballs, because his eye would be on the ball when it was 15 to 25 feet from the plate, and his depth perception and line of sight information would warn him of an inaccurate model. Thus he could update his mental model as shown in the last 150 ms of Figure 64c.

To generalize this theory what would happen if the batter *overesti*mated the speed of the pitch? The batter would perceive the ball dropping more than expected in the last few feet. The ball would break so fast it would look "like it rolled off a table." Such fast breaking curves have been described by professional batters. However, in Chapter 2 we showed that the curve ball exhibits a continuous curve and not an abrupt break near the plate. Now, we can explain this seeming contradiction. The apparent, abrupt break of a curve ball is probably due to the batter's overestimation of the speed of the pitch for his mental model.

It would be impossible to hit the ball if it really did jump or break just before the plate. For example, a foul tip changes the ball's trajectory abruptly in the last few feet before the catcher and the umpire. As a result these masked men cannot predict the ball's trajectory and they must wear protective clothing.

To summarize our theory, we think every pitch (knuckle balls expected) follows a smooth trajectory. The apparent, abrupt jumps and drops right before the plate are perceptual illusions, caused by the batter using the optimal learning strategy of tracking and having mistakes in his mental model of the pitch.

To summarize the implications of our theory, we think that in the first third of the ball's flight, the batter forms his mental model of the ball's trajectory. In the middle third, he observes differences between the actual trajectory and his mental model, updates his mental model, and finalizes his swing. In the last third, he observes errors in his mental model so that he can track the next pitch better.

◆ *Generalizations* ◆

Our findings should generalize to other sports. In tennis, for example, the distances are similar, 60.5 ft for baseball and 78 ft for tennis, as are the linear velocities, 100 mph for a fast pitch and 110 mph for a fast serve. There is often a change in the ball's trajectory just before the player hits it: the baseball curves and the tennis ball bounces. Tennis coaches, even more than batting instructors, teach beginners to use the strategy with the anticipatory saccade in order to see the ball hit the racket; this strategy is probably only useful as a learning tool. Therefore, we suggest that neither baseball players nor tennis players keep their eyes on the ball. The success of the good players is due to faster smooth pursuit eye movements, a good ability to suppress the vestibulo-ocular reflex, and the occasional use of an anticipatory saccade.

Sometimes our subjects used the strategy of tracking with head and eyes but also using an anticipatory saccade, and sometimes they used the strategy of tracking with head and eyes and falling behind in the last 5 ft. Len Matin of Columbia University has speculated that athletes might use the former strategy when they are learning the trajectory of a new pitch and the latter strategy when hitting home runs.

Notes

1. A. T. Bahill and T. LaRitz, "Why Can't Batters Keep Their Eyes on the Ball?," *American Scientist*, vol. 72, 1984, pp. 249–253. Original source of data showing how close to the plate a batter can follow the ball.

2. T. Williams and J. Underwood, *The Science of Hitting*, Simon and Schuster, New York. 1982. An explanation of how he did it, by one of the best hitters of all time.

3. F. Frohlich and G. R. Scott, "Where Spectators Sit to Catch Baseballs," *Baseball Research Journal, Tenth Annual Historical and Statistical Review of the Society for American Baseball Research*, vol. 10, 1981, pp. 132–138. A hard-to-find paper showing where 1000 fair and foul balls landed in the Astrodome in 57 games.

4. A. T. Bahill and J. S. Kallman, "Predicting Final Eye Position Halfway Through a Saccade," *IEEE Trans. Biomed. Engr.*, vol. BME-30, 1983, pp. 781–786. An engineering study of the inter- and intra-subject variability of human saccadic eye movements.

5. J. D. McDonald, A. T. Bahill, and M. B. Friedman, "An Adaptive Control Model for Human Head and Eye Movements While Walking," *IEEE Trans. Syst. Man. Cybern.*, vol. SMC-13, 1983, pp. 167–174. The first study showing eye movements while walking. It also presents a model for eye-head-body coordination while walking.

6. R. D. Lyons, "Take Your Eye Off the Ball, Scientist Coaches Sluggers," *New York Times*, science section, June 12, 1984, pp. 19 and 23. A layman's explanation of the Bahill and LaRitz paper.

7. L. Stark, J. A. Michael, and B. L. Zuber, "Saccadic Suppression: A product of the Saccadic Anticipatory Signal, in C. R. Evans and T. B. Mulholland, (eds.), *Attention in Neurophysiology*, Butterworths, London, 1969, pp. 281–303. The term saccadic suppression first appeared in this paper. It gives an explanation of why we cannot see our eyes move when we look between the images of our eyes in a mirror.

8. E. Matin, "Saccadic Suppression and the Dual Mechanism Theory of Direction Constancy," *Vision Res.*, vol. 22, 1982, pp. 335–336. A psychophysical explanation of why we cannot see our eyes move when we look between the images of our eyes in a mirror.

9. J. Brinkman, and C. Euchner, *Umpire's Handbook*, Steven Greene Press, Lexington, Mass. 1987. Helpful advice for umpires.

10. A. T. Bahill and J. D. McDonald, "Model Emulates Human Smooth Pursuit System Producing Zero-Latency Target Tracking," *Biol. Cybern.*, vol. 48, 1983, pp. 213–222. The mental model used for visual tracking of moving objects.

11. A. T. Bahill and J. D. McDonald, "Smooth Pursuit Eye Movements in Response to Predictable Target Motions," *Vision Res.*, vol. 23, 1983, pp. 1573–1583. Eye movements of humans tracking moving targets. This contains the data used to make the mental model for eye tracking.

12. J. D. McDonald and A. T. Bahill, "Zero-Latency Tracking of Predictable Targets by Time-Delay Systems," *Int. J. Control*, vol. 38, 1983, pp. 881–893. The mathematics of the mental model for visual tracking of moving targets.

13. D. Regan, K. I. Beverley, and M. Cynader, "The Visual Perception of Motion in Depth," *Scientific American*, vol. 241, no. 1, 1979, pp. 136–151. An simple explanation of visual perception of motion in depth.

Physiological Predictors of

Batting Performance

any physiological parameters can be used to predict whether or not a particular ball player will be successful. To start with it is helpful if the player is big, strong, and fast. Professional teams already measure such parameters. But there are many other quantitative parameters that they could use.

Visual acuity is important for a batter. Ted Williams had 20/10 visual acuity; such acuity is possessed by about one in a thousand people in the 20- to 30-year age bracket. However, there are now more sophisticated

---

Most of this chapter was based on McHugh and Bahill.[1] 1985.

measures of visual acuity, for example, contrast sensitivity and dynamic visual acuity. To measure acuity a person looks at letters on a chart and tries to identify them. In a test of contrast sensitivity the subject is presented a series of sine wave gratings, which look like the alternating black and white bars shown in Figure 65, and is examined to determine the closest spacing of bars that the subject can perceive. In a test of dynamic visual acuity a letter is projected on a screen 10 feet in front of the subject. The letter is rotated clockwise starting at 100 rpm. The rotational speed is gradually decreased, and the fastest speed at which the subject can identify the letter is recorded. (This is much like trying to read the label on a rotating phonograph record. Most people can read the label at 33 rpm; few people can read it at 78 rpm.) Data collected from over 800 subjects showed that Olympic-caliber baseball players had better static visual acuity and contrast sensitivity than age-matched nonathletes, but their superiority in the dynamic visual acuity tasks were not statistically significant.[2,3] Tests of contrast sensitivity are more complicated and more time consuming than tests of static visual acuity, but they yield additional information that may be of predictive value.

Optometric exams given to the members of the 1984 U.S.A. Olympic volleyball team have shown big intrasubject differences in depth perception, in ability to track moving objects, and in ability to not suppress vision in one eye or the other. Getz says these differences correlate with performance.[4,5]

Another physiological trait that may be correlated with good performance has to do with preference of hand and eye usage. Most humans are right handed, although some are left handed, and a few are ambidextrous. Coincidentally most humans are also right-eye dominant. To determine your eye dominance point to an object across the room; first close one eye and then the other. Whichever eye keeps your finger on the object is your dominant eye.* Your finger pointing at the object across the room can only be aligned with one of your eyes. You point with your dominate eye: for most people that is their right eye. However, right-handedness does not imply right-eye dominance. Although most people are right handed and most people are also right-eye dominant, there is no cause-and-effect link. Now comes the crux of our discussion: in the field of baseball, several investigators[6] have demon-

---

*If the results of this experiment are equivocal, then instead of pointing with only one hand, form a small hole between your hands, then raise both arms straight out in front of you. Sight an object across the room as before, and close first one eye then the other. Whichever eye allows you to see the object is the dominant eye.

FIGURE 65. *A sine wave grating like those used to test contrast sensitivity. The bars on the left are easier to discriminate because they are wider and are more widely spaced than the bars on the right.*

strated that batters who are right handed and left-eye dominant or left handed and right-eye dominant (called cross dominant) have statistically higher batting averages than noncross dominant players. Although this result is statistically significant, there are no explanations for it: it is a correlation, and not a cause and effect. For example, some reasons suggested for the advantage of cross-dominant batters are that they have the dominant eye 2 inches closer to the pitcher, and that it is the batter's dominant "eye that is facing the pitcher"; these explanations are ridiculous. The best we can say is that cross-dominant batters have statistically higher batting averages. The cause is probably wrapped up in the complexity of the human brain, and the different capabilities of each half of the brain.

Bat speed and consistency of swings are important for batting success. These parameters are already considered by the scouts. The equipment and experiments mentioned in Chapter 5 would help quantify these observations.

THE CALTECH THEORETICAL BASEBALL TEAM PRACTICING FOR THE BIG GAME

Quickness is another important parameter in determining potential for success. Quickness is easy to identify but hard to define. Coaches easily identify their quick players. But when asked to explain why they call these players quick, they waffle. Their uneasy verbalizations include phrases like they react quickly, they move fast, they steal a lot of bases, they get into position to field the ball quickly, they swing the bat fast, and they beat out bunts. However, all of these phrases describe results not physiological characteristics. However, we think there are physiological parameters that can be measured to determine quickness. In particular, we believe that the force-velocity curves of Chapter 5, the latency of the saccadic eye movement system, and eye-hand reaction time can be used to quantify quickness. Quick players had large slopes on the force-velocity curves presented in Chapter 5. Saccadic eye movement latency can be measured with standard tests in any oculomotor laboratory. Eye-hand reaction time can be measured in the following way:

1. Holding a meterstick in front of a subject. Instructing him or her to straddle the 50-cm mark with the index finger and thumb and to watch the fingers of the experimenter, who is holding the end of the meterstick.
2. When the experimenter opens his fingers, and the meterstick begins to fall, the subject should grasp the stick between the finger and thumb.
3. The place on the meterstick where the subject catches it is an indication of eye-hand reaction time.

Thus quickness can be measured and we think it will correlate with success playing baseball.

Many laboratories are studying the movement of athletes by digitizing television camera images with computers.[7,8] Commercially available systems cost $50,000 to $300,000. These systems record the data from a $1/4$- to 2-second movement in a computer. With digital reconstruction they can display a three-dimensional representation of the movement with millisecond resolution. These movements can be replayed at any speed or viewing angle, and the trajectories of individual limbs and joints can be compared to the trajectories of an expert template. Sometimes this expert template is that of a widely recognized world champion, and sometimes it is derived from the movements of the same athlete when he or she was in top form. Such studies can help an athlete change his or her motion to conform to that of the expert template and thus increase performance. Because these studies are so time consuming and expensive, they have not yet been used to predict potential, but rather they have mostly been used to help correct the movements of already highly skilled athletes.

Our final example of physiological parameters that could be measured to predict batting performance, which we will pursue in great detail, is the ability to learn to track novel visual targets. Subjects who have this ability to learn tracking of novel waveforms are more likely to be better hitters.

◆ Good Batters Quickly Learn to Track Novel Visual Targets ◆

Every human movement system has a time delay of about 200 milliseconds (ms). To see the effects of this time delay hold a dollar bill between someone's outstretched finger and thumb. Tell him he can have the dollar if he can catch it. Then drop it. The 200-ms time delay will prevent the subject from grasping the dollar bill. The human eye tracking system has a similar time delay. But humans can overcome this time delay and track predictable targets with no delay, provided the target position waveform is smooth, is predictable, has frequencies between 0.1 and 1.0 Hz, and has small accelerations. However, it takes time to learn this zero-latency tracking. In this section we show the time course for learning to track a particular target waveform. And we show that professional baseball players learn to track faster than typical college students.

We measured eye movements with the photoelectric system discussed in the last chapter. However, in this study we eliminated vergence eye movements by putting the targets on a curved screen in front of the subject, and we eliminated vestibulo-ocular eye movements by immobilizing the subject's head with a head rest and a bite bar. Also, the bandwidths for the data of this chapter were larger, with the position and velocity bandwidths being 80 and 9 Hz, respectively. The subjects were two dozen male and female college students, and three members of the Pittsburgh Pirate Baseball Club.

The visual target was a little red dot of light projected on a white screen in front of the subject. This dot moved leftward then rightward and the subject tried to track it, in much the same way the subject would do so seated on the net line while trying to follow the ball in a tennis match. This dot of light moved back and forth with a cubical target position waveform (shown in Figure 66). We used this waveform because no naturally occurring visual targets move with a cubical waveform. Thus, our results were not influenced by prior learning. However, the position trace of the cubical waveform looks like the familiar sinusoid (most natural movements are sinusoidal; for example, if you jump on the bumper of a car, it will bounce up and down in a sinusoidal manner), but the velocity is strikingly different. Therefore, by analyzing the eye velocity records we could tell if the subject had really learned the cubical waveform, or if he had merely approximated it with a sinusoid. The cubical target waveform is described by the equation

$$r(t) = 10.39 \, A[2(t/T)^3 - 3(t/T)^2 + (t/T)] \qquad \text{for } 0 < t < T$$

where T represents target period and A is the amplitude. Previous studies have shown that humans track well when the target has an amplitude of 5 degrees and a frequency of about 0.33 Hz (a 3-s period), and so these values were used in our experiments.

Our experiments began with a 6-s calibration target waveform (where the target jumped abruptly between two points 10 degrees apart), followed by 9 s of the cubical target waveform, 3 s of the calibration target waveform, another 9 s of the cubical waveform, and finally another 6 s of the calibration target waveform. The subjects were allowed to rest for 5 minutes and then the sequence was repeated. This process continued for about 2 hours.

Our metric for how well each subject tracked the target was the mean squared error (mse) between the eye and target positions. For each 9-s epoch of the cubical waveform, we averaged the mean squared errors for the left and right eyes and plotted this average as a function of the amount of time the subject had seen the target, as shown in Figure 67. Exponential curves were fit to the mean squared error data. The best fit was usually an exponential of the form

$$\text{mse} = Ae^{-Bt} + C$$

We called these exponential equations *learning curves*.

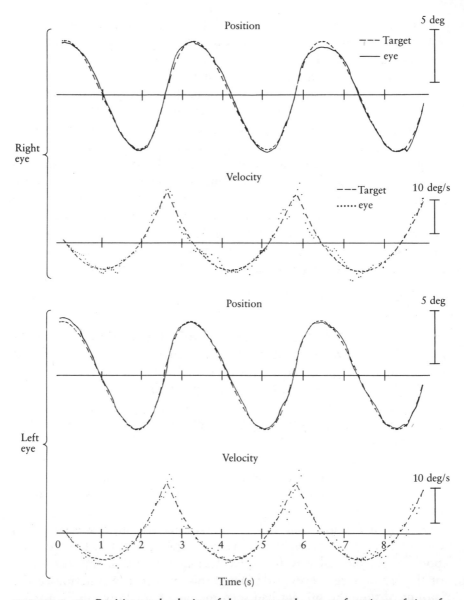

FIGURE 66. *Position and velocity of the target and eyes as functions of time for good tracking of a cubical waveform. Upward movements in this figure represent rightward movements. [From D. E. McHugh and A. T. Bahill,* Invest. Ophthalmol. Vis. Sci., *26:932–937, 1985.]*

FIGURE 67. *Time course of learning the cubical target waveform for two subjects. Mean squared error (mse) is plotted against the total time that the subject had seen the waveform. Circles are the human data points and the solid line is an exponential curve fit to the data points. [From D. E. McHugh and A. T. Bahill, Invest. Ophthalmol. Vis. Sci., 26:932–937, 1985.]*

◆ *Learning Curves* ◆

Figure 67 shows learning curves for two subjects. The circles represent the human mean squared error, the solid line is the best exponential fit to the data. For the lower graph the equation for this exponential fit is

$$\text{mse} = 0.42e^{-0.26t} + 0.05$$

To give some feel for what these numbers mean, assume that the fovea (the center part of the retina that has good acuity) has a radius of 0.5 degree. Now if the target were always just on the edge of the fovea, then the mean squared error would be $(0.25 \text{ deg})^2$. Figure 67 shows that in the beginning the subjects were not keeping their foveae on the target, whereas at the end they were keeping the target centered on their foveae. Figure 66 shows an example of a well-practiced subject keeping the target centered on his foveae. For this figure the mean squared error between the eye and target was $(0.06 \text{ deg})^2$.

The solid lines of Figure 68 show the learning curves fit to the data of our four best students. The correlation between the exponents and the steady-state values was -0.19. Therefore, there seems to be no relationship between how fast the subject learned and how low of a mean squared error was reached in steady state.

We were trying to quantify the ultimate capabilities of the human smooth-pursuit system, and so we only report the performance of our better subjects. In this chapter we only show data of 4 of our 24 students. The other students did not demonstrate such low error tracking. We note in passing that our female subjects did not track as well as our male subjects.

To zero in on optimal human performance we decided to study optimal humans. Who is an optimal human? For eye tracking capability we thought professional athletes would fit the bill. So, we invited some professional athletes to participate in our experiments. The mean squared errors for three members of the Pittsburgh Baseball Club are represented by solid circles, open circles and open squares in Figure 68. In viewing the target for the first time, baseball players 2 and 3 had much smaller mean squared errors, $(0.08 \text{ deg})^2$ and $(0.05 \text{ deg})^2$, than our other subjects. They had never seen a cubical waveform before, yet they started out with low mean squared errors. Three years after these data were collected baseball players 2 and 3 were playing for the Pittsburgh Pirates and the Saint Louis Cardinals, respectively. Player number 1 was

FIGURE 68. *Time course of learning for seven subjects. Solid lines are the expo-nential learning curves fit to the data of our four best students. Circles and squares are data points for three professional athletes. The professional baseball players learned the waveform faster than the students. [Adapted from D. E. McHugh and A. T. Bahill, Invest. Ophthalmol. Vis. Sci., 26:932–937, 1985.]*

still playing class A ball in the Pittsburgh Farm System. These data seem to indicate that the ability to track the cubical waveform is correlated with athletic performance. However, we caution that our sample was small.

Why should it be important for baseball players to learn new wave-forms quickly? In a typical game a batter might see a particular pitch at most two dozen times. Given that a pitch takes about one-half of a second, he would see the ball in flight for only a dozen seconds each game. Therefore, we should be studying only the first one or two data points of Figure 68, which is the region where the professional athletes excelled.

After a batter learns a pitch, does he retain that knowledge? The data of Figure 69 suggest that he does. Figure 69 shows the mean squared

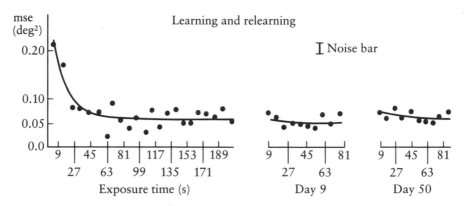

FIGURE 69. *Time course for learning and relearning. The subject learned the waveform, returned 9 days later to relearn, and returned 50 days after the original experiment to relearn it again. Once people learn a certain trajectory, whether it is the trajectory of a laser beam in a laboratory or the trajectory of a pitched ball, they remember it for a long time. [From D. E. McHugh and A. T. Bahill,* Invest. Ophthalmol. Vis. Sci., *26:932–937, 1985.]*

errors for one student during the initial learning session, for a session 9 days later, and for a session 50 days later. For each session the data were fit with an exponential curve. Relearning was almost instantaneous. It appears that the cubical target waveform was not quickly forgotten. Which suggests that the batter can also remember the trajectory of a particular pitch for a long time. Rookie pitchers and those traded from one league to another often have a period of phenomenal success. However, after they have been around a while, the batters have learned the trajectories of their pitches and the honeymoon is over.

In the laboratory we study humans learning to track sinusoidal, parabolic, and cubic waveforms. This correlates with baseball players on the field learning to track fastballs, curve balls, and sliders.

◆ *Differences Between the Eyes* ◆

Humans can track certain targets very well, as shown in Figure 66. Using only smooth-pursuit eye movements, this subject was able to keep his fovea on the target for over 9 s. Saccades were not removed or filtered out of these eye position traces; indeed small conjugate saccades can be seen at the 8.5-s mark. Please note that there are differences between the movements of the right and the left eye, as can be seen in the position traces between the 6 and 7 second marks. Comparison with the data between the 3 and 4-second marks shows that these differences are of biological origin and are not due to instrumentation errors. Differences of this magnitude between the right and left eye were typical of our data. The dominant eye did not track better than the nondominant eye; the errors were of the same magnitude. So these data show that normally there are small differences in the tracking of our two eyes; but humans are not aware of it, and, therefore, it is not significant. This means that eye tracking capabilities provide no advantage or disadvantage to being right-eye dominant and right handed, or right-eye dominant and left handed, or vice versa.

◆ *Generalizations* ◆

From this study we draw the following conclusions: (1) There are differences between the tracking of the two eyes, but neither eye is consistently better. (2) Professional baseball players have better tracking abilities than our best students; specifically, they learn to track novel targets in less time.

These tests of learning to track the cubic waveform could be used in screening baseball players in the major league farm system. It could provide one more tool for evaluating potential; it could show which players have the requisite oculomotor coordination to be good hitters and which do not.

Notes

1. D. E. McHugh and A. T. Bahill, "Learning to Track Predictable Target Waveforms Without a Time Delay," *Invest. Ophthalmol. Vis. Sci.*, vol. 26, 1985, pp. 932–937. A study of human learning in an eye-tracking task.
2. B. Coffey and A. W. Reichow, "Guidelines for Screening and Testing the Athlete's [Visual System]," *Optometric Extension Program Foundation Curriculum II*, vol. 59, no. 7, April 1987, pp. 47–60. A protocol for optometric exams of athletes.

3. B. Coffey and A. W. Reichow, "Athletes vs. Nonathletes: Static Visual Acuity, Contrast Sensitivity, Dynamic visual acuity," *ARVO Abstracts*, vol. 19, 1989, p. 517. A preliminary report of their data.

4. D. J. Getz, "Vision and Sports," *J. Am. Optometric Assoc.*, vol. 49, 1978, pp. 385–388. An optometric study of Olympic volleyball players.

5. J. Hansen, "For Their Eyes Only," *Volleyball Monthly*, May 1983, pp. 23–25.

6. J. M. Portal and P. E. Romano, "Patterns of Eye-Hand Dominance in Baseball Players," *New England J. Medicine*, vol. 319, 1988, pp. 655–656. A short summary of data gathered from a college baseball team.

7. B. Cramblitt, "Computers Capture Moments of Motion," *Computer Graphics World*, March 1989, pp. 50–58. Explanation of computer-TV camera systems for studying motion of nonbaseball athletes.

8. Anonymous, "Science Is Changing the Old Ball Game," *Compressed Air Magazine*, April 1989, pp. 12–18. Explanation of computer-TV camera systems for studying movements of baseball players.

Baseball Batting Statistics: Were Yesterday's Players Better?

Every baseball fan knows that nobody has batted .400 since Ted Williams turned the trick in 1941. During the 1986 season, only seven players in the combined National and American leagues had batting averages exceeding .300. Is this because the old-timers were better hitters? Is it because more hitters today are swinging for the fences? Are modern-day pitchers better?

First, let's look at the data. Figures 70, 71, and 72 show us that both the game and the players have changed over the years. The number of double plays per game has increased somewhat, and the number of errors per game decreased markedly over the years (Figure 70). This implies that the abilities of fielders have improved. Figure 71 shows that

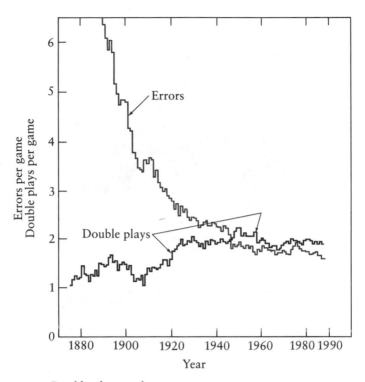

FIGURE 70. *Double plays and errors per game.*

both the number of home runs per game and the number of strikeouts per game have increased. Both began their most recent steady increase in the 1920's, and strikeouts appear to have leveled off since about 1960. Home runs per game have recently begun another increase. Because these changes are in close correlation, the "swinging for the fences" theory of increased home run production gains credence. Batting averages and earned runs per game, on the other hand, have remained relatively constant over the years (Figure 72). To be sure, there have been periods of increase and decrease in these figures, but, ultimately, batting averages hover around .260 and earned runs per game remain close to 3.8. In 1941, when Ted Williams batted .406, the average batting average in the combined major leagues was .262 and 3.89 earned runs were produced per game. Perhaps this means that Williams was far better than the average player of his day, while George Brett, admittedly a superstar, is not quite so far above today's average player. Baseball fans, however, still like to ask the ultimate question: Were Ty Cobb,

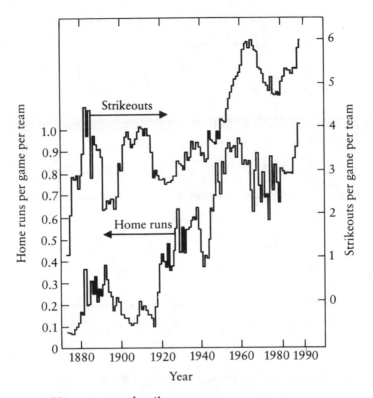

FIGURE 71. *Home runs and strikeouts per game.*

Babe Ruth, and Ted Williams better hitters than, say, George Brett, Rod Carew, and Wade Boggs?

Thorn and Palmer[1] have described a technique for making such comparisons, concluding that many of the best modern-day players would have been superstars of even greater proportions had they played the game 50 years before with the same abilities they possess today. Thorn and Palmer pointed to a study by Cramer[2] where a method was suggested for comparing the batting skills of players in different years. Cramer calculated the Batter Win Average, a measure of runs produced above the average divided by the number of plate appearances by the player. He then converted these results to predicted batting averages. Cramer's method leads to some astonishing predictions, as pointed out by Rubenstein.[3] For example, the "real" lifetime batting averages of yesteryear's stars are very low. While George Brett and Rod Carew had "real" lifetime batting averages of .341 and .325 (the best of the group),

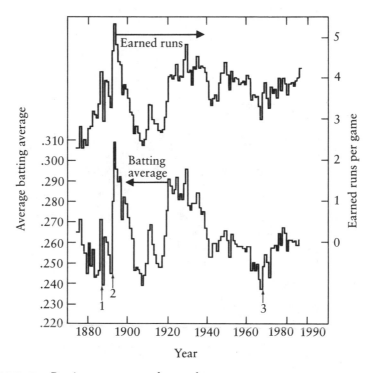

FIGURE 72. *Batting averages and earned runs per game.*

Ty Cobb batted only .289 and Babe Ruth, a paltry, .262. Rubenstein predicted that "the problem with these statistics is that no one will believe them." Should they? Rubenstein[3] further stated:

> Dallas Adams has pointed out to me (that) the table of "corrections" Cramer has compiled apply to an entire league in a particular season, not to a particular player. And while one might well have to subtract 101 points from the batting average of a mediocre American League hitter in 1921 to arrive at his 1976 batting average, is it really true of the Ty Cobbs and George Sislers? Evidence that it is not so seems implied in the well-documented fact that the gap between the average league batting average and the league-leading batting average has been consistently narrowing throughout the century: in 1911, for instance, Cobb's batting average exceeded the American League average by 137 points, but most recent batting champs have exceeded their league batting average by only 60 to 70 points. It thus seems that the very best hitters of the past were very much better than the average hitters

of their day. Because of this, Cramer's "corrections" probably cannot be applied to all players of the past: they almost certainly cannot be applied to the very best players of former ages.

This is a jewel of insight. "Average" hitters of today may be very much better than "average" old-timers, but perhaps the very best players of both eras are comparable in skill.

Gould[4] has recently proposed a remarkably simple and, at first glance, counterintuitive explanation of the demise of the .400 hitter by proceeding precisely along the line of reasoning first expounded by Rubenstein. Gould claims that while the best players of today are neither appreciably better nor worse than the best of the old-timers, there are more very good players now. But wouldn't this mean more, rather than fewer, .400 hitters? The theory requires some explanation.

"I'M SORRY, ROGER, BUT YOU'VE REACHED THE MANDATORY RETIREMENT BATTING AVERAGE OF .150."

Records are made to be broken. There is little doubt that athletes get better over the years. People in general are healthier and bigger than they were 50 years ago. There are also more people actively competing in various sports than there were in the not too distant past. To see that the top athletes get better and better one only needs to look at the record book for Olympic sports like running, jumping, throwing, and swimming. Today, the sub–four minute mile is commonplace. Before the mid-1950's it was considered a virtual impossibility. As a specific example of how athletic improvement has occurred over the years, consider the Boston Marathon. In 1922, Clarence DeMar ran the Boston Marathon in 2:18:10, a record that stood for 34 years, when Aniti Viskari of Finland ran the 26-mile distance in 2:14:14. Today, the record stands at 2:07:51, a mere 7.5 percent improvement over DeMar's time. In the years between 1921 and 1956 there were some remarkably slow race winners (Figure 73). In 1931 the winning time was 2:46:45.8. Since 1969, no winning time has been above 2:19. Only runners who have run a marathon in less than 3:30 during the previous year are allowed to

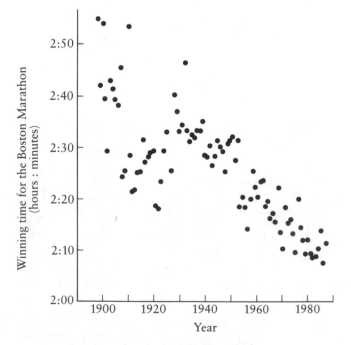

FIGURE 73. *Running times for the Boston Marathon.*

participate in the race. Thousands qualify. Scores of runners finish in less than 2:25 each year.

The conclusion seems clear. The very best runners today, in spite of vast improvements in training techniques, diet, equipment, etc., are better, but not tremendously better, than the best runners of 50 or 60 years ago. As any serious road racer will testify, however, there are many more exceptionally good runners.

Now, baseball is a very different sport from running. In racing, the athlete is pitted against the clock. To be sure, other people are involved, and the aim is to defeat them, but one is not allowed to interfere with their efforts. The faster and stronger a runner is, the more likely he is to win and to set a new record. In baseball, things are different. The batter's job is to hit the ball and to reach base safely. The pitcher's job (along with that of his teammates) is to make the batter's job as difficult as possible. If it makes sense that the skill of the average batter should have improved over the years, then it makes as much sense that the skill of the average pitcher has also improved. Which has improved more? (As a former pitcher, I [RGW] must admit that it seems to me that pitching appears to have a historic tendency to dominate the game, but this is not important.) What is important is that whenever one side, offense or defense, begins to hold the upper hand and to rule the game, the spectators begin to lose interest and the owners change the rules to restore equilibrium.

Baseball is a finely tuned sport, and only the most delicate adjustments are required to bring the game into balance when it strays. In fact, one can easily recognize the effects of rule changes in Figure 71 and 72. Some rule changes that produced detectable changes are listed in Table 12. The simple bookkeeping change of not counting a base on balls as a hit, for example, shows up dramatically. The rule was instituted in 1888, and the average batting average dropped from .271 the previous year to .239 (see the first arrow in Figure 72). The following year the number of balls necessary to walk a batter was decreased from seven to four. The number of walks per nine innings increased from 2.21 in 1888 to 3.46 in 1889. The pitcher also had to "groove" the ball in order to avoid walking even more batters, and batting averages responded by increasing to .263.

In 1893, the pitching distance was increased from 50 feet to 60.5 feet. Batting averages increased from .245 in 1892 to .290 in 1893 (second arrow in Figure 72) and to .309 in 1894. They then began a slow downward drift. Spitball pitching began, and perhaps knuckle balls and other trick pitches were also introduced. Pitchers slowly began to domi-

TABLE 12 Some Rule Changes over the Years

1888	Strike out on 3 strikes instead of 4.
	Base on balls not counted as a hit.
1889	Base on balls on 4 balls instead of 6.
1893	Pitching distance moved from 50 ft to 60.5 ft.
1894	Batter charged with strike for foul bunt.
1895	Bat diameter increased from 2.5 to 2.75 in.
	Strike charged for foul tip.
1903	Pitcher's mound no higher than 15 in.
1909	Foul bunt on third strike is a strikeout.
	Cork centered ball introduced.
1920	Spitball abolished (actually gradually).
1926	Sacrifice fly introduced.
	Ground rule double.
1940	No sacrifice fly.
1954	Sacrifice fly reintroduced.
1963	Strike zone enlarged.
1969	Strike zone shrunk.
	Pitcher's mound lowered to 10 in.

nate. By 1908, the average batting average had dropped to .239 and the number of earned runs per game had dipped from 5.32 in 1894 to 2.37. In an effort to stem the tide, the cork-centered ball was introduced near the end of the 1909 season. The hitters responded by batting .250 and scoring an average of 2.78 earned runs per game in 1910, and these numbers climbed to .269 and 3.37 by 1912. But by 1918 they had again dropped. In that year, the batting average was .254 and only 2.77 earned runs were scored per game. Something else had to be done.

In 1919, the use of the spitball and other trick pitches like the shine ball and the emery ball were prohibited. Actually, the rule did not take effect until the 1920 season, and even then a "grandfather clause" was adopted, first allowing each team to name two spitball pitchers for the 1920 season and then, in 1921, allowing eight National League and nine American League pitchers to use the pitch for the remainder of their careers. Hitting dominated for the next 10 to 20 years, with batting averages hovering around .285 and earned runs per game between 4.0

and 5.0. In 1930, the average batting average was .296 and teams earned an average of 4.81 runs per game. Home runs per game skyrocketed from 0.23 in 1918 to 1.26 in 1930.

By 1940, the pitchers were beginning to come into their own again. In 1955, hitters batted .259 and produced only 4.00 earned runs per game. By 1968, these numbers had fallen to .237 and 2.98. The owners began to get nervous. The 1969 season began with two major rules changes in place. The strike zone was to include only the area between the armpit and the top of the knees (it has previously been from the top of the shoulders to the bottom of the knees) and the height of the pitcher's mound was lowered from 15 inches to 10 inches.

The response was immediate. The average major league batting average rose to .248 in 1969 (third arrow in Figure 72) and to .254 in 1970. Earned runs per game rose to 3.62 and then to 3.89. The numbers jumped again slightly in 1977 when the American League introduced the designated hitter, but have otherwise remained fairly constant.

If seemingly minor rule changes are reflected in average performances, how do these show up in the performances of individuals? Every individual is different, of course. Ted Williams, Ty Cobb, Rod Carew, and Wade Boggs were all different people with different personalities who played the game in different home parks under different conditions and against different opponents. We will argue, as did Gould, that a reasonable measure of an individual hitter's performance in a given year is the number of standard deviations above the league average the hitter batted during that year.

The argument, elaborated by Gould,[4] is as follows: Suppose the abilities of the very best players is invariant, or nearly invariant, from player to player over different eras. These are the Cobbs and the Bretts of any era. The rest of the players making up a league have abilities spread over a spectrum. Suppose we are to select 500 players to make up a baseball league. The larger the pool from which the players are drawn, the narrower will be the spectrum of abilities. Imagine, for example, a society so large that it could produce an entire league of players who could bat as well as Ty Cobb. If every player had an average year, the league batting average would be, say, .360, and the range of batting averages would be zero. Everyone would hit .360. If the rules were now changed to favor the pitcher sufficiently to bring the league average down to .260, there would, of course, be no .300 hitters, only an entire league full of .260 hitters.

In the real world, of course, the abilities of hitters in the major leagues is still spread over a spectrum. The talent pool has, however, increased over the years for a variety of reasons. In addition to population growth itself, the entry of Blacks, Mexicans, Puerto Ricans, and others has considerably increased the potential number of outstanding players. One might therefore expect a decrease over time in the range of batting averages in a given year in the major leagues. Such a decrease has, in fact, occurred.

We have calculated the means and the standard deviations for each of the major leagues from each league's inception through 1987. The results are shown as Tables 13 and 14. We used data tabulated by Reichler.[5] In performing the calculations, only players having at least two at-bats per game on the average were included, so that the results would reflect the abilities of "regular" players. Gould has kindly provided us with the results of a similar calculation that he performed, including players with at least one at-bat per game. Gould's results are in parentheses in Tables 13 and 14. His calculated standard deviations are somewhat larger than ours, reflecting the fact that players with between one and two at-bats per game were of marginal ability. The trends in the two sets of results are quite similar. Along with considerable year-to-year scatter, one does see the expected gradual decrease in standard deviation with time.

When we do statistical analyses, the larger the group of subjects, or tests, the more meaningful the analysis becomes. Generally, when the number of subjects is very large, the data begins to look like a standard distribution and the standard deviation takes on a specific meaning. In simple terms, about 68 percent of all the subjects fall within the range of one standard deviation about the average, 95 percent fall within two standard deviations, and 99.7 percent fall within the range of three standard deviations. A batter might be considered to have an outstanding year if his average places him more than two standard deviations above the league average. If he hit more than three standard deviations above the average, he would qualify as a genuine superstar. The number of standard deviations n above the league average that an individual player achieved can be calculated using the simple formula

$$n = \frac{\text{individual batting average} - \text{league batting average}}{\text{standard deviation for that year}}$$

In calculating n, we used the league batting average, as tabulated in Tables 13 and 14, rather than that compiled by Reichler.[5] This league batting average as well as the standard deviation therefore reflect "regular" players—those who batted two or more times during an average

TABLE 13 National League		
Year	Mean	Standard Deviation
1876	.26547	.04976
1877	.27540	.04783
1878	.25934	.05210
1879	.25612	.04837
1880	.24855	.03998
1881	.26264	.04386
1882	.25813	.04097
1883	.26485	.04163
1884;*	.25294	.04353
1885	.25343	.04693
1886	.26340	.04794
1887	.27808	.03963
1888	.25245	.03665
1889	.27649	.03678
1890;**	.26418	.03547
1891	.26263	.02919
1892	.25809	.03301
1893	.29065	.03647
1894	.32098	.04147
1895	.30764	.04302
1896	.30424	.03971
1897	.30188	.04178
1898	.28188	.03740
1899	.29949	.03793
1900	.29353	.03593
1901	.28590	.04491 (.0474)
1902	.27056	.03920 (.0443)
1903	.28537	.03535 (.0393)
1904	.26343	.03121 (.0375)
1905	.27280	.03476 (.0382)
1906	.25884	.03575 (.0368)
1907	.25763	.02933 (.0305)
1908	.25308	.03120 (.0342)
1909	.25726	.03141 (.0349)
1910	.26829	.02854 (.0328)
1911	.27367	.03255 (.0361)
1912	.28824	.02747 (.0361)
1913	.27667	.02597 (.0281)
1914	.26731	.02852 (.0310)
1915	.26186	.02594 (.0292)
1916	.26189	.02820 (.0318)
1917	.26458	.02638 (.0298)
1918	.26913	.02889 (.0365)
1919	.27737	.02390 (.0359)
1920	.28150	.03039 (.0339)
1921	.30495	.02993 (.0344)
1922	.30548	.03119 (.0381)
1923	.29928	.03265 (.0349)
1924	.29492	.03375 (.0352)
1925	.30805	.03167 (.0333)
1926	.29593	.02831 (.0367)

(continued)

TABLE 13 National League (continued)		
Year	Mean	Standard Deviation
1927	.29569	.02974 (.0338)
1928	.29807	.03448 (.0352)
1929	.31062	.03515 (.0397)
1930	.31715	.03591 (.0389)
1931	.29176	.03265 (.0357)
1932	.29137	.03190 (.0359)
1933	.28134	.03106 (.0337)
1934	.29267	.02969 (.0308)
1935	.29112	.03061 (.0290)
1936	.29279	.0335 (.0341)
1937	.28355	.03912 (.0368)
1938	.27872	.02802 (.0289)
1939	.28605	.02717 (.0312)
1940	.27939	.02879 (.0328)
1941	.27230	.02904 (.0329)
1942	.26202	.02621 (.0304)
1943	.26948	.03233 (.0362)
1944	.27637	.03187 (.0343)
1945	.27969	.02719 (.0312)
1946	.27113	.02869 (.0303)
1947	.28115	.02512 (.0328)
1948	.27566	.02968 (.0341)
1949	.28236	.02680 (.0317)
1950	.28053	.02765 (.0306)
1951	.27748	.02820 (.0334)
1952	.26703	.02876 (.0324)
1953	.28217	.03240 (.0347)
1954	.28241	.03324 (.0360)
1955	.27496	.02868 (.0319)
1956	.27063	.02858 (.0315)
1957	.27498	.02829 (.0339)
1958	.27875	.02871 (.0314)
1959	.27828	.02689 (.0311)
1960	.27180	.02453 (.0308)
1962	.27592	.02787 (.0295)
1963	.26141	.03164 (.0324)
1964	.27057	.03093 (.0326)
1965	.26630	.02815 (.0334)
1966	.27388	.02603 (.0316)
1967	.26717	.03360 (.0370)
1968	.25870	.02916 (.0311)
1969	.26607	.03170 (.0350)
1970	.27517	.03380 (.0342)
1971	.26779	.03340 (.0344)
1972	.26481	.03197 (.0348)
1973	.27088	.02895 (.0344)
1974	.27117	.02652 (.0303)
1975	.27379	.03204 (.0348)
1976	.27275	.03088 (.0377)
1977	.27611	.02557 (.0312)

TABLE 13 National League (continued)		
Year	*Mean*	*Standard Deviation*
1978	.26945	.02489 (.0305)
1979	.27352	.02638 (.0303)
1980	.27021	.02540 (.0315)
1981	.26991	.03132 (.0315)
1982	.27089	.02342 (.0361)
1983	.26934	.02531
1984	.26864	.02614
1985	.26840	.02525
1986	.26623	.02815
1987	.27853	.02616

*Union Assoc.: .26116; .05019.
**Player's League: .28449; .04321.

game. Table 15 is a summary of the results. This table lists all those players whose batting average in a given year was more than three standard deviations above the league average.

The first two entries will not surprise baseball aficionados. Napoleon Lajoie's *n* of 3.934 occurred when he hit .422 during 1901 when the American League average was .290 and the standard deviation was 0.034. In 1924, Rogers Hornsby batted 3.825 standard deviations above the National League average. The third, fourth, and fifth entries will surprise many. Because both batting averages and standard deviation have been generally low in recent years, an individual player's batting average need not reach the lofty heights of the .400 hitters of earlier days to be more than three standard deviations above the league average. Both George Brett and Rod Carew turned the trick while batting in the .380's while Wade Boggs' .368 placed him third on the all-time best single season list. In fact, Carew appears on the list three more times, with batting averages of "only" .364, .359, and .350. Boggs appears four times in six years, and missed a fifth year only very narrowly.

Table 15 contains a smattering of players from all eras. This is essentially by design, of course, since our initial assumption was that the best players of every era were about equal in ability. Note, however, that some of the great players of the past are surprisingly absent. Conspicuous for its absence is the name of "Shoeless" Joe Jackson, who compiled a lifetime batting average of .356, batting .408 in 1911 and .395 in 1912. The trouble is that during those two years, the American League batting

TABLE 14 American League			
Year	Mean	Standard Deviation	
1882	.24880	.04717	
1883	.25869	.03629	
1884	.25490	.04130	
1885	.25713	.04299	
1886	.25663	.03773	
1887	.28402	.04430	
1888	.24788	.03658	
1889	.27110	.03784	
1890	.26880	.04648	
1891	.26601	.03845	
1901	.29003	.03355	(.0389)
1902	.29110	.03662	(.0421)
1903	.26905	.03612	(.0399)
1904	.25593	.03459	(.0360)
1905	.25183	.03114	(.0363)
1906	.26395	.03680	(.0438)
1907	.26142	.02917	(.0381)
1908	.25045	.02856	(.0328)
1909	.26053	.03693	(.0372)
1910	.26175	.03371	(.0424)
1911	.29293	.04351	(.0483)
1912	.27998	.04100	(.0424)
1913	.27708	.03860	(.0411)
1914	.26495	.03519	(.0382)
1915	.26446	.03576	(.0371)
1916	.26281	.03633	(.0354)
1917	.26087	.03946	(.0398)
1918	.27269	.03803	(.0391)
1919	.28260	.03539	(.0398)
1920	.29766	.03906	(.0431)
1921	.30541	.03208	(.0430)
1922	.29990	.03583	(.0373)
1923	.29518	.03875	(.0431)
1924	.30547	.03110	(.0354)
1925	.30610	.03897	(.0435)
1926	.29658	.03495	(.0366)
1927	.30097	.03679	(.0366)
1928	.29702	.03286	(.0369)
1929	.29872	.03429	(.0363)
1930	.30917	.03490	(.0393)
1931	.29564	.03311	(.0346)
1932	.29182	.03048	(.0344)
1933	.28592	.02994	(.0336)
1934	.29878	.02968	(.0371)
1935	.29319	.02516	(.0321)
1936	.30340	.03307	(.0357)
1937	.29707	.03252	(.0371)
1938	.29502	.02890	(.0335)

Year	Mean	Standard Deviation	
TABLE 14 American League (continued)			
1939	.29542	.02800	(.0318)
1940	.28434	.03298	(.0355)
1941	.28194	.03401	(.0365)
1942	.27466	.02727	(.0321)
1943	.26067	.02593	(.0303)
1944	.27428	.02721	(.0314)
1945	.27035	.02413	(.0298)
1946	.27420	.03338	(.0346)
1947	.27059	.03052	(.0349)
1948	.27954	.03195	(.0320)
1949	.27835	.02599	(.0298)
1950	.28437	.03193	(.0314)
1951	.27613	.02583	(.0340)
1952	.26860	.02630	(.0270)
1953	.27476	.02569	(.0302)
1954	.27012	.03084	(.0319)
1955	.27398	.02893	(.0365)
1956	.27453	.03272	(.0346)
1957	.27012	.03441	(.0344)
1958	.27409	.02857	(.0332)
1959	.26756	.03058	(.0309)
1960	.27268	.02149	(.0268)
1961	.27349	.02665	(.0293)
1962	.26855	.02629	(.0300)
1963	.26022	.02381	(.0269)
1964	.26330	.02360	(.0272)
1965	.25635	.02553	(.0285)
1966	.25457	.02246	(.0276)
1967	.25043	.02760	(.0306)
1968	.24827	.02634	(.0333)
1969	.26596	.02467	(.0305)
1970	.26301	.02983	(.0318)
1971	.26579	.02534	(.0306)
1972	.25593	.02606	(.0306)
1973	.26709	.02650	(.0295)
1974	.26450	.02764	(.0283)
1975	.26624	.02818	(.0325)
1976	.26348	.02850	(.0310)
1977	.27243	.03115	(.0325)
1978	.26980	.02227	(.0293)
1979	.27476	.02834	(.0289)
1980	.27772	.02965	(.0324)
1981	.26116	.03016	(.0326)
1982	.27194	.02625	
1983	.27101	.02956	
1984	.26979	.03012	
1985	.26763	.02636	
1986	.26852	.02838	
1987	.27181	.03005	

TABLE 15			
Player	*Year*	*Batting Average*	n
N. Lajoie	1901	.422	3.934
R. Hornsby	1924	.424	3.025
W. Boggs	1985	.368	3.808
G. Brett	1980	.390	3.787
R. Carew	1977	.388	3.710
T. Cobb	1910	.385	3.656
T. Williams	1941	.406	3.648
N. Lajoie	1910	.384	3.627
N. Lajoie	1904	.381	3.616
H. Stovey	1884	.404	3.610
R. Carew	1974	.364	3.600
T. Gwynn	1987	.370	3.497
T. Williams	1957	.388	3.426
T. O'Neill	1887	.435	3.408
T. Speaker	1916	.386	3.391
S. Musial	1948	.376	3.381
G. Sisler	1922	.420	3.352
W. McGee	1985	.353	3.350
R. Carew	1975	.359	3.292
N. Cash	1961	.361	3.284
G. Musial	1946	.365	3.272
H. Walker	1947	.363	3.258
R. Barnes	1876	.429	3.256
H. Wagner	1908	.354	3.235
T. Cobb	1912	.410	3.171
T. Cobb	1909	.377	3.154
T. Gwynn	1984	.351	3.151
H. Wagner	1907	.350	3.149
R. Carew	1973	.350	3.129
W. Boggs	1986	.357	3.118
W. Keeler	1897	.432	3.114
C. Anson	1881	.399	3.109
T. Cobb	1917	.383	3.095
R. Garr	1974	.353	3.086

TABLE 15 (continued)			
Player	Year	Batting Average	n
R. Hornsby	1921	.397	3.076
T. Cobb	1922	.401	3.073
A. Vaughn	1935	.385	3.067
R. Hornsby	1922	.401	3.063
J. Dimaggio	1939	.381	3.056
H. Zimmerman	1912	.372	3.049
W. Boggs	1983	.361	3.044
T. Cobb	1907	.350	3.037
W. Boggs	1987	.363	3.035
F. Dunlap	1884	.412	3.005

averages were .293 and .280, and the standard deviations were 0.044 and 0.410. Even Ty Cobb's .420 batting average in 1911 placed him less than three standard deviations (2.920) above the league average. Hugh Duffy's all-time high batting average of .438 in 1894 does not qualify for Table 15. Three other players also hit .400 or better during that year. The National League batting average was .321 and the standard deviation 0.041. Hitting three standard deviations above the league average would have required a player to bat .446!

We have not yet computed lifetime statistics of most of the players. We have done this for 10 players in Table 16: Wade Boggs, Tony Gwynn, George Brett, Rod Carew, Ty Cobb, Rogers Hornsby, "Shoeless" Joe Jackson, Napoleon Lajoie, Babe Ruth, and Ted Williams. Although Brett appears fourth on the all-time best single season list, his lifetime average value of n is "only" 1.513. Jackson has no single season better than 3.000, but his consistency helped him to gain a 2.054 lifetime n. Babe Ruth was a slugger. The quantity 1.311 does not, of course, accurately reflect his value as a hitter. As a power hitter, he was without peer.

Carew and Hornsby show 2.125 and 2.230 over fairly long careers, while Williams has an impressive 2.137, showing considerable consistency over a career interrupted by two wars. The most impressive num-

TABLE 16 Lifetime Statistics for 10 Players									
Ty Cobb		Rod Carew		Nap Lajoie		Babe Ruth		Ted Williams	
YEAR	N	YEAR	N	YEAR	N	YEAR	N	YEAR	N
1906	1.523	1967	1.506	1897	1.463	1918	0.718	1939	1.128
1907	3.037	1968	0.903	1898	1.233	1919	1.113	1940	1.809
1908	2.572	1969	2.677	1899	2.123	1920	2.006	1941	3.648
1909	3.154	1970	1.626	1900	1.460	1921	2.263	1942	2.983
1910	3.656	1972	2.382	1901	3.934	1922	0.421	1946	2.031
1911	2.920	1973	3.129	1902	2.045	1923	2.524	1947	2.373
1912	3.171	1974	3.600	1903	2.380	1924	2.332	1948	2.8
1913	2.925	1975	3.292	1904	3.616	1925	−0.413	1949	2.487
1914	2.928	1976	2.369	1905	2.478	1926	2.158	1950	1.022
1915	2.923	1977	3.710	1906	2.474	1927	1.496	1951	1.621
1916	2.978	1978	2.838	1907	1.288	1928	0.791	1954	2.428
1917	3.095	1979	1.526	1910	3.627	1929	1.350	1955	2.835
1918	2.874	1980	1.797	1911	1.656	1930	1.428	1956	2.154
1919	2.865	1981	1.454	1912	2.147	1931	2.336	1957	3.426
1920	0.930	1982	1.793	1913	1.501	1932	1.614	1958	1.887
1921	2.606	1983	2.300	1914	−0.197	1933	0.504	1959	−0.443
1922	2.822	1984	0.837	1915	0.435	1934	−0.363	Career	2.137
1923	1.157	1985	0.469	1916	−0.463	Career	1.569		
1924	1.046	Career	2.125	Career	1.813				
1925	1.845								
1926	1.214								
1927	1.523								
1928	0.791								
Career	2.372								

TABLE 16 Lifetime Statistics for 10 Players (continued)									
George Brett		*Rogers Hornsby*		*Joe Jackson*		*Wade Boggs*		*Tony Gwynn*	
YEAR	N	YEAR	N	YEAR	N	YEAR	N	YEAR	N
1974	.633	1916	1.812	1911	2.645	1982	2.936	1982	.733
1975	1.482	1917	2.366	1912	2.805	1983	3.044	1983	1.567
1976	2.439	1918	0.411	1913	2.485	1984	1.833	1984	3.151
1977	1.270	1919	1.700	1914	2.076	1985	3.808	1985	1.925
1978	1.087	1920	2.912	1915	1.218	1986	3.118	1986	2.230
1979	1.914	1921	3.076	1916	2.192	1987	3.035	1987	3.497
1980	3.787	1922	3.063	1917	1.017	Career	2.962	Career	2.184
1981	1.752	1923	2.595	1919	1.933				
1982	1.107	1924	3.825	1920	2.159				
1983	1.319	1925	2.998	Career	2.054				
1984	0.472	1926	0.744						
1985	2.556	1927	2.196						
1986	0.757	1930	—						
1987	0.605	1931	1.202						
Career	1.513	Career	2.230						

bers for those having completed long careers belong, as might be expected, to Ty Cobb. For one thing, his career spanned 23 years. Between 1906 and 1922 he hit less than 2.6 standard deviations above his league average only once. For consistent batting excellence over an extended period of time, Cobb was apparently without peer. There can be little doubt that he was the greatest hitter of all time.

But watch out for Wade Boggs! During Cobb's first six seasons he batted, on the average, 2.810 standard deviations above the league average. To date, Wade Boggs is hitting an astonishing 2.962 standard deviations above the American League average. If he continues at this pace, he may well replace the Georgia Peach as the greatest hitter of all time.

Notes

1. J. Thorn and P. Palmer, *The Hidden Game of Baseball*, Doubleday, New York, 1984. Lots of interesting data and the authors' own methods of calculating who the best players were.

2. R. Cramer, "Average Batting Skill Through Major League History," *Baseball Research Journal*, 1980. One writer's opinion on how to compare different batters from different eras.

3. W. Rubinstein, "Commentary on 'Average Batting Skill Through Major League History,'" *Baseball Research Journal*, 1981. Interesting rebuttal to Cramer's method of comparing batters.

4. S. J. Gould, "Why No One Hits .400 Any More," *Discover*, vol. seven, August 1986. Delightful insights by a lover of baseball and science.

5. J. L. Reichler, *The Baseball Encyclopedia*, 7th edition, Macmillan, New York, 1988. All the statistics you need and more.

INDEX